"Combining pastoral, missional, ؛
fully explores the little understooɑ
Christians affirm and the new creatiↄ ….. …… ……ɔy. ɪne result is *Not Home Yet*, a book with rich discussion of the interconnections of Scripture's earliest and future themes and profound encouragement for all those who are still on their way to the home that Jesus Christ prepares for us."

Bryan Chapell, Pastor, Grace Presbyterian Church, Peoria, Illinois

"*Not Home Yet* is a compact and powerful exposition of the Bible's teaching on earth and God's mission to it. I have never seen such a clear articulation of the theme of creation and re-creation anywhere. Ian Smith also deftly speaks about the practical ramifications that such a teaching has on our thinking and our actions. I highly recommend this book for all who are serious about understanding this central theme of the Bible."

Tremper Longman III, Distinguished Scholar and Professor Emeritus of Biblical Studies, Westmont College; author, *Confronting Old Testament Controversies*

"When we are away from home, we long for home. But where is home for the Christian? In this insightful biblical theology of 'home,' Ian Smith helps us see that this world, and even heaven (as an intermediate state), is not our home—we're just passing through, as we await our eternal home of the new heavens and the new earth. A great book to be read for the journey home."

Jonathan Gibson, Assistant Professor of Old Testament, Westminster Theological Seminary

"*Home* must surely be one of the most emotion-filled words in the English language. It is where we belong. But where is home for the Christian? Are we living in a far country here on earth, just waiting for a better day when we can leave the earth and simply enjoy heaven? Think of Ian Smith as your friendly theological realtor. He knows about the home God has created for us. With theological skill and deft simplicity, he can explain its long history. He understands where we fit into its story. He is also sensitive to the responsibility Christians have to our 'home,' even though we have not yet seen its final reconstruction. Brief as *Not Home Yet* may be, you will find it instructive and challenging beyond its size."

Sinclair B. Ferguson, Chancellor's Professor of Systematic Theology, Reformed Theological Seminary; Teaching Fellow, Ligonier Ministries

"Ian Smith's book will give you new insight into old passages, let you ponder all that is packed into Jesus's resurrection, and get you dreaming of the new heavens and the new earth."

Ed Welch, Faculty and Counselor, Christian Counseling & Educational Foundation

"*Not Home Yet* is theologically rich yet easily accessible for anyone. Smith paints a vivid picture of how this earth matters to God—our work, our communities, and the physical world—things that some have often said are passing away and don't have eternal value. I highly recommend this insightful and much-needed book."

Scott B. Rae, Dean of Faculty and Professor of Christian Ethics, Talbot School of Theology, Biola University

"Ian Smith has written an eminently readable account of the biblical testimony to our eternal home—a home with resurrection bodies in a renewed heaven and earth. His careful analysis of common but ill-informed references to 'going home' as merely a departure from this earth, rather than a return to a renewed earth, are clear, cogent, and well argued. This concise biblical theology of death, afterlife, and resurrection should be an encouragement to every Christian reader as they grasp the fullness of the hope that awaits the people of God."

Glenn N. Davies, Archbishop of Sydney; author, *Faith and Obedience in Romans*

"When will we arrive home? That's an emotive question, often asked in the most vulnerable experiences of our lives—when we are children, separated from loved ones, or approaching death. Answering this theological question requires exegetical precision and pastoral sensitivity. Ian Smith is a careful reader of Scripture, a gifted preacher and communicator, and a compassionate pastor. In *Not Home Yet*, he guides us on a journey from Eden through a world that, in its fallen state, is not our home. But the central figure in this guide book is the Lord Jesus Christ, who came to bring about a new creation."

Gregory R. Perry, Vice President of Strategic Projects, Third Millennium Ministries

"Christians have a particular understanding of the world we live in because we believe that it has been created by God. We must take care of it. Ian Smith provides a theological underpinning for the kinds of actions that are required if we are to fulfill our creation mandate. This book is an important contribution to a necessary debate, and I recommend it highly to all who have a serious interest in the subject."

Gerald Bray, Research Professor of Divinity, Beeson Divinity School

Not Home Yet

Not Home Yet

How the Renewal of the Earth Fits
into God's Plan for the World

Ian K. Smith

WHEATON, ILLINOIS

Library of Congress Cataloging-in-Publication Data

Names: Smith, Ian K., author.
Title: Not home yet : how the renewal of the earth fits into God's plan for the world / Ian K. Smith.
Description: Wheaton, Illinois : Crossway, 2019. | Includes bibliographical references and index.
Identifiers: LCCN 2018056844 (print) | LCCN 2019016833 (ebook) | ISBN 9781433562785 (pdf) | ISBN 9781433562792 (mobi) | ISBN 9781433562808 (epub) | ISBN 9781433562778 (pbk.) | ISBN 9781433562808 (epub)
Subjects: LCSH: Creation. | Restoration ecology. | Redemption—Christianity. Second Advent. | Home—Religious aspects—Christianity.
Classification: LCC BT695.5 (ebook) | LCC BT695.5 .S643 2019 (print) | DDC 231.7—dc23
LC record available at https://lccn.loc.gov/2018056844

Crossway is a publishing ministry of Good News Publishers.

VP   29   28   27   26   25   24   23   22   21   20   19
15   14   13   12   11   10   9   8   7   6   5   4   3   2   1

Lovingly dedicated to Jenni
"According to his promise we are waiting for new heavens
and a new earth in which righteousness dwells." (2 Pet. 3:13)

Contents

Introduction

Traveling is fun, but after a while we long for home. We enjoy exotic food and hotel rooms, but when homesickness takes hold, we hunger for a home-cooked meal, and we yearn to sleep in our own bed. Home is where we belong. It's a place of familiarity. In the light of this, the practice of many Christians calling heaven their home is curious. Heaven is not a place of familiarity. It's an unknown. Is it where we belong? There are heavenly creatures, angelic beings around the throne of God. But that's not us. We are earthly creatures. Yet at funerals we talk about the deceased having been called home. When going through difficult times, we remind each other that this world is not our home. But if heaven is our home, what does that say about the earth? Humans were given the task of filling the earth and having dominion over it (Gen. 1:28).

Where Is Home?

There is an element of truth in the claim that heaven is home, and we will return to that later in this book. Christians are at home when we are with Christ, as we await Jesus's return to the earth. We will be "at home with the Lord" (2 Cor. 5:8). But the Scriptures also talk about the renewal of all things (Matt. 19:28), a new heaven and a new earth (Rev. 21:1). How does this home in heaven fit with the renewal of the earth? What is the home of Christians beyond the grave? What impact does an understanding of the resurrection of Jesus have on the way we see the earth? Where is home?

The resurrection of Jesus points to something far bigger than just access to heaven; the resurrection points to the renewal of God's creation. When we understand this scope of God's work of salvation, reductionistic and individualistic views are lacking in the grandeur of what God is going to do. Jesus's resurrection does not only guarantee my resurrection—important though that is. Jesus is going to raise the universe! He will usher in a new heaven and a new earth, and we will be part of that. On that day, we will know what it means to be home. This salvation is guaranteed through the resurrection. To talk about salvation without mention of the resurrection is a serious omission.

This connection between the resurrection and the renewal of creation is not as well understood as one might hope. I sit on several panels that assess people's suitability for various forms of Christian ministry. We interview people who are desiring to be ordained ministers, missionaries, evangelists, and similar roles. Within the interview, we always ask the interviewee for an explanation of the gospel. In nearly every answer, I notice two things—one good and one concerning. First, virtually without exception, the person mentions the cross as a place of forgiveness and substitution. This is encouraging. The second thing I notice over 90 percent of the time is that within the summary of the gospel, there is no mention of the resurrection. I normally ask, "Have you left anything out?" The candidate sits and ponders. Around half of those being interviewed say, "Ah—the resurrection." Others need more prompting. I then proceed to ask whether the resurrection is important. They all say yes. Most can cite: "And if Christ has not been raised, then our preaching is in vain and your faith is in vain" (1 Cor. 15:14). I then ask, "Why is it important?" Answers vary. Many make good theological observations, but very few link the resurrection with the renewal of all things. Normally an understanding of the gospel is individualistic; it's about *my* salvation.

The resurrection is central to how we see salvation. We are not saved just for a purely spiritual experience in heaven. Jesus was raised to earth, not to heaven. We should not confuse the resurrection and the ascension. The Gospels all agree that on the third day, Jesus was raised to earth where he continued to appear for forty days before his ascension to heaven. This resurrection of Jesus is the firstfruits of our resurrection. A physical body was placed in the grave of Joseph of Arimathea and was raised back to life. The grave was empty. The very same body was raised. This is the firstfruits of the general resurrection (1 Cor. 15:20, 23). We too will be raised—our very same body. The earth will be raised—the very same earth. In each case there will be transformation, but there will also be continuation.

Yet when I find myself in conversations with Christians talking about the renewal of the earth, they look at me quizzically and wonder what Bible I've been reading. So ingrained is the idea of living in heaven forever that questions arise. The most frequent is addressed by this book: Is this idea of a renewed earth biblical? In this book we will work our way through Scripture and show that the resounding answer is yes. We will note repeatedly that the Bible is more concerned with God coming down to earth than with humans going up to heaven. This downward movement is seen in Eden, in the tabernacle, in the temple, in the incarnation, in the crucifixion, in the resurrection, and in the second coming. Jesus's return to this earth is the focus of the Christian's hope, and this return will not just be for a visit, to pick us up and take us home to heaven. He is coming to stay. The new Jerusalem will descend to earth (Revelation 21), and we will be at home, with Jesus, on earth.

The Future of the Earth

An understanding of the future of the earth has significant implications for how we see it now. When we understand that the end of all things is the renewal of all things, then all things become important. No longer will we see the spiritual as more important than the physical; such a dualism is more indebted to Greek philosophy than to the Bible. God is committed to his creation. It's all important, whether Bible study, employment, church, hobbies, family, the arts, or community involvement. When we understand that the impact of the resurrection is much bigger than we ever imagined, our worldview will be changed. No longer will our sermons be just about what happens after death (important though that is), the gospel will also resound with relevance to this life, to the earth, to the places we inhabit and call home. The knowledge that our home will be renewed will give relevance to life.

The aim of this book is to reawaken (resurrect even), a biblical understanding of the earth and God's mission to it. Such an understanding was common in former generations, but it has waned over the decades. The evolution of Christian music is but one example of this. Isaac Watts's hymn "Joy to the World" was written in 1719, and it celebrates God's commitment to this earth as heaven and nature sing the blessings of Jesus's incarnation as far as the curse is found. The cry of Watts's hymn is, "Let earth receive her King."[1] Unfortunately, such songs are rare today, as Christians often celebrate the earth's destruction and an eternal home in heaven (I refrain from citing examples,

1. Isaac Watts, *The Psalms and Hymns of Isaac Watts: With All the Additional Hymns and Complete Indexes*, Great Awakening Writings (Morgan, PA: Soli Deo Gloria, 1997), 173.

but there are many—just listen to what you are singing next Sunday). If our understanding of Christian mission has been reduced to "getting people into heaven," what does that say about people's physical needs? What is the purpose of Christian schooling? What is the relationship between education and evangelism? Why do we have Christian hospitals, especially on the mission field in developing countries? If the main purpose of a Christian hospital is to get people into heaven, we have a bit of a problem! One could argue that the job of a hospital is to delay entry to heaven! Is there a place for the physical in our understanding of salvation?

The need to be reminded of our earthly as well as our heavenly focus has never been as urgent. In the West the Christian church has moved, in one generation, from being the most powerful voice in society to being a superseded voice at the fringes. Christendom is over. For many the church has become irrelevant. I often ask myself, *Which happened first? Did the world forsake the church or did the church forsake the world?* No wonder the world sees Christians as irrelevant, if everything on earth is transient.

Of course, questions abound. Didn't Jesus say, "My kingdom is not of this world" (John 18:36)? Didn't Paul say, "For me to live is Christ, and to die is gain" (Phil. 1:21)? Isn't the earth going to pass away? As we trace the flow of the biblical story, we will look at broad themes, and we will stop along the way to take a closer look at some difficult passages. In all of this we will be reminded of God's commitment to our home. After all, he made it.

It has taken me some time to get my head around how holistic God's mission is to this world (and I certainly do not claim to have it all sorted out). Like many Western Christians, I grew up in a world of physical affluence and spiritual poverty.

Everyone at my school ate three meals a day, wore shoes, and could read and write, but very few went to church. We were physically rich and spiritually poor. In a very real sense, the proclamation of the gospel addressed a spiritual need. But not all the world is like that. This truth came home to me after teaching for several years in a theological seminary in the small Pacific Island nation of Vanuatu. Most people in Vanuatu are subsistence farmers. The church is strong and influential, but the country is financially poor. After my family had lived there for about five years, one of our graduates, Johnny, invited us to visit him. He was pastoring in an extremely remote part of the country, on the west coast of the island of Santo in the village of Sulesai. We had always enjoyed spending time with Johnny and his family, so we accepted with pleasure. It would be a great adventure to take the whole family to a part of the world that is very inaccessible and by and large unchanged by Western influences.

We set out early in the morning before the sun had risen. We bounced along a rough dirt road in the back of a truck for two hours, traversing fast-flowing rivers, until we reached the west coast of the island, where we boarded a small aluminum dinghy with an outboard motor and set off for a ten-hour trip up the coast in the open sea. From the boat it is easy to see why this part of the world is so isolated. Soaring mountains drop through sheer cliffs to the ocean floor, making the coast absolutely impassable. There are only two ways in and out. For those who have money, there is the boat, but for most people who are subsistence farmers in a cashless economy, the only way in and out is across steep, mountainous terrain, a walk that takes three or four days. It's no surprise that many people are born, live, and die in this part of the world without ever leaving, and that visitors seldom come.

At the end of a long day, we arrived at Sulesai village, picturesque in its tropical beauty. A freshwater river wends its way through the village before disgorging into the ocean; the green of the jungle contrasts with the blue of the ocean, each separated by the pebbles of the seashore. Children ran to the beach to greet us, and in my romanticized naivety I thought: "Who would ever want to leave this place?" How naive I was!

As we came ashore, I noticed that most of the children had distended bellies, a telltale sign of malnutrition. This made no sense in a tropical paradise, but the availability of food does not always lead to good nutrition. Several of these children's parents and grandparents were amputees through the complications of untreated diabetes. Medical facilities are all but nonexistent in a place that is plagued with malaria. Mosquito repellent cannot be purchased. The rate of infant mortality is high. Childbirth is precarious. There is no school in the village; parents face the decision of whether to send their six-year-olds to boarding school, from which they will return annually. It is not surprising that many people in the village are illiterate. The place looked like paradise, but there was a sting in its tail.

As we came ashore, Johnny led us to the simple church building in the middle of the village. The church in Sulesai is different from any church I have visited (and I am talking about the people, not the building). Every person in the village belonged to it. Yes—everyone! Not only did it have a 100 percent attendance rate, but they met daily. Due to high levels of illiteracy, the people of Sulesai gathered every morning to have the Bible read to them and to pray together before beginning their day's work. *Everyone* attended *every* day. As far as the human eye can see, everyone professed to be a Christian. No need for a program on church growth in Sulesai! Yet as I stood, amidst them, with their medical, nutritional, and educational needs,

I asked myself, *Is there still Christian ministry to be performed here? Do they need missionaries?* This place was in absolute juxtaposition to where I grew up. In Sulesai everyone went to church, but very few ate three meals a day, wore shoes, or could read and write. What was more urgently needed here— a nutritionist or an evangelist? Questions flooded my mind. Is not the Christian mission holistic? Was not the resurrection of Jesus physical? Is caring for people a vehicle to enhance the proclamation of the gospel, or do we proclaim God's love by our actions as well as our words? The answers to my questions came home with astounding clarity.

That day at Sulesai demonstrated the three main truths I want to address in this book: (1) the earth is stunningly beautiful; (2) the earth is marred by the effects of sin; (3) God is concerned for the renewal of the earth. None of these truths deny the centrality of the call of the gospel for people to repent and to put their trust in Jesus. That is always foundational. But once we've done that, it's not the end of the story. A spiritual gospel that is concerned only for spiritual realities ends up being a gospel that falls far short of what the Bible teaches. Real spirituality is holistic. The story of the Bible is concerned with God's commitment to fix up earth, a place called "home." We turn our attention to tracing that story.

1

The Creation of Home

The first chapter of the Bible is Genesis 1. That seems such a bland statement, but its ramifications are enormous. Starting our Bible with creation, rather than with the fall in Genesis 3 or with the call of Abraham in Genesis 12, will make a world of difference (sorry about the pun). A true appreciation of the beginning of the biblical narrative will help to prevent a false dichotomy between the spiritual and the physical. It will correct many misconceptions about heaven, about the earth, and about the relationship between them. The opening chapters of Genesis teach us that earth is our home.

In the Beginning

The opening words of Scripture, "In the beginning God created the heavens and the earth" (Gen. 1:1), remind us that God is the Creator and not part of his creation. This distinction makes us reject any notion of pantheism, with creation having its own internal force. We do not venerate "Mother Earth" or the power of nature. Our world is created and sustained by the hand of God, who is separate from it yet committed to it.

The words "the heavens and the earth" (Gen. 1:1) need definition. In the worldview of the ancient Near East, all that existed was categorized as "the heavens" that are above, "the earth" that is below the heavens, and "the waters" that are around and beneath the earth. This division can be seen in the Ten Commandments given to Moses. In the second commandment Moses was told, "You shall not make for yourself a carved image, or any likeness of anything that is in the heaven above, or that is in the earth beneath, or that is in the water under the earth" (Ex. 20:4). A paraphrase of the first verse of the Bible could be, "In the beginning, God created everything."[1]

The Hebrew for "the heavens" is *hashamayim*. Its meaning should not be restricted to that other-worldly dimension where God and his angels reside. It includes all that is above the earth. It is the place where birds live (Ps. 8:8), from where the dew (Gen. 27:28), the wind, and the rain (Jer. 10:13) come. We could translate these references as "sky," as long as we recognize that this is not the extent of "the heavens." The heavens also include what we would call "space." The sun, the moon, and the stars are in the heavens. Abraham is promised descendants as numerous as the stars of heaven (Gen. 15:5). All that is above, in short, can be included in the heavens.

All this raises a question about what we often call "heaven," that is, where God lives surrounded by his angels. Is that included in the heavens? The short answer is yes, although the ancient reader of Genesis would not have divided what we call "sky" from what we call "space" from what we call "heaven." Indeed, it is hard to quantify the biblical idea of heaven as God's

1. Gordon J. Wenham, *Genesis 1–15*, vol. 1, Word Biblical Commentary (Nashville: Thomas Nelson, 1987), 15.

abode. It is where God lives, yet it is unable to contain him (1 Kings 8:27; 2 Chron. 2:6; 6:18). It is a "place" to which one ascends (Ps. 139:8; Prov. 30:4) and from which God descends (Gen. 11:5; 2 Sam. 22:10; Pss. 18:10; 144:5), yet it cannot be reached either by plane or by rocket. In short, the heavens are all that is above. We should be careful not to import our own questions or categories onto the text if those questions are not addressed by the text. One thing we do know about the heavens: they are God's creation!

Similarly, the Hebrew for "the earth" in Gen 1:1 (*ha'arets*) has more than one meaning. As with the English word *earth*, it can mean not only the planet upon which we live but also the soil in which things grow (Gen. 1:26). It is from the dust that Adam was made (Gen. 2:7), and the earth continues to feed and nourish us. But *ha'arets* has a more particular meaning than just the earth: it is a reference to the land which God promised to the patriarchs, whose family would become the nation of Israel (Deut. 1:8), a good land flowing with milk and honey (Ex. 3:8). Again, to ask questions of subcategories between the earth and the land may not always do justice to the text. Although Genesis is clearly the story of the creation of the earth, it is also the creation of the land. Similarly, we will notice that by the end of the story of the Bible, when we talk about the "Holy Land," we are also talking about the "Holy Earth," as God's blessings will flow to the ends of the earth (Acts 13:47).

In short, the opening verse of the Bible is breathtaking: "In the beginning, God created the heavens and the earth." From this all-encompassing canvas, the focus of Genesis narrows: "The earth . . ." (Gen. 1:2). This begins what will become a recurrent pattern of the earthward direction in Scripture. The earth appears to be at the center of God's creation. Even the sun and the moon exist for the benefit of dividing time on the earth between day and night. It is an anti-Copernican revolution; everything revolves around the earth.

Commitment to Creation

The astute reader cannot help but grasp the pleasure that God takes in the earth. The world is not just a functional, monochrome, utilitarian machine. It is full of beauty, color, and creativity. God delights in the trees, the fish, the animals, the oceans, and the mountains. At the end of each day of creation, the Lord looks at what he has made and declares it to be "good" (Gen. 1:4, 10, 12, 18, 21, 25). The Hebrew word used here for "good" (*tob*) can also be rendered "beautiful." On the sixth day of creation, God's looking at all he has made and declaring it to be "very good" could equally be rendered "very beautiful" (Gen. 1:31). The very same Hebrew expression is found in 1 Samuel 9:2 to describe how handsome Saul was, and in Genesis 24:16 to describe the beauty of Rebekah, who came to a well to collect water before becoming Isaac's wife. Similarly, God looks at the world he has made and says, "It's stunningly beautiful." Not everything needs to be useful; beauty is an end in itself. God takes great delight in it, as should we. Earth is our home, and except for the all-pervasive effects of sin, it is hard to imagine anywhere better. God did not hold back when he created this world by keeping the best for heaven. The biblical narrative tells us that he is not going to allow Satan to have the final victory as far as this beautiful world is concerned. Earth will not be discarded. Creation is more valuable than that; it will be renewed.

Of course, the world is not all that we would want it to be. Suffering pervades every part of our lives, and for most people the heartache is palpable. We will deal with the effects of the fall in the next chapter. The question we face now is: In terms of God's beautiful creation, what is the solution to the problem of evil? Will God fix up our home (the earth), or will we need to flee to a new home (heaven)? It is a similar issue that many people in the twenty-first century encounter, as they are faced with terrible atrocities in some of the war-torn countries of the world. Should they stay, or should they flee from their homes? With growing numbers of refugees around the world, we must remember that fleeing one's homeland is normally a last resort. People have lived in their homelands for generations. They have developed a culture, a language, and a heritage, and such traditions are not easily abandoned. Indeed, even if people flee and start a new life in another country, they still think about home and try to keep alive its language and traditions. After all, there is nothing physically wrong with their homeland. Many of the trouble spots in the world are places of great beauty and fertility. But due to the effects of evil, the people who live there are faced with a difficult choice: stay and fix it up or flee and start a new life somewhere that is not home. The preferred solution is to stay, but that is not always possible.

This question also faces us as we think about God's creation. Is the world so broken that God will abandon it, and we will need to find a home elsewhere? Is heaven a place for eternal refugees, that we might live in a home that was not made for us (unless we are angels)? The recurring answer of both Testaments of Scripture is that the world is not so broken that God cannot fix it. It will be renewed and transformed. God is not going to give up on it, and neither should we. It's good to remember that the New Testament's image of salvation is often given in creational terms. Language such as "new creation" (2 Cor. 5:17; Gal. 6:15) is supplemented with a picture of creation being subjected to the pains of childbirth as it awaits something better (Rom. 8:22).

The focus of the creation account in Genesis continues to narrow as the narrative zooms in to a particular garden called "Eden." This garden is where God dwells with his people on earth. It has all that we would expect to find within a temple in the ancient Near East. A temple was the earthly dwelling place of a god where humans met with their god, and within which were found images of the god. But Eden is a temple with a difference. It is not a static, lifeless building. It is a dynamic, growing garden. God is not a lifeless statue within this temple, but he walks and talks within the garden (Gen. 3:8). The same is also true of his images within the temple. Unlike lifeless statues in other ancient temples, God's image bearers are living. They are not made of wood or stone but of flesh and blood. Their names are Adam and Eve. They are made in their God's image, and they are to rule over all that God has made (Gen. 1:26–27). It is a temple *par excellence.*

All later tabernacles and temples within the history of the people of Israel will be but a reflection of Eden. The garden of Eden is the exemplar of what it looks like when heaven and earth meet. Within this temple, God has bestowed purpose to his image bearers: to have vice-regal authority as they manage development in God's world. Adam and Eve were created to "be fruitful and multiply and fill the earth and subdue it, and have dominion over the fish of the sea and over the birds of the heavens and over every living thing that moves on the earth" (Gen. 1:28). This is why humans were created. It goes to the core of our reason for existence. We were not created to preach the gospel, important though that is. Such a conclusion assumes that the Bible begins with the fall in Genesis 3. The Bible begins at Genesis 1. We are image bearers whose function is to act on behalf of the king with vice-regal authority as we care for his creation.

I am an Australian, and vice-regal authority is reflected in our political system. Although not an absolute monarch, as is the case with God, Australia's head of state lives in London, and so a governor-general represents her (or him, as the case may be) within Australia. This vice-regal system goes back to the time of European settlement in 1788 when a colony consisting mainly of convicts was established in Sydney. At that time King George III was the king in London. His image was on money, and his insignia was engraved on public buildings. But engraved images are unable to rule a colony of convicts on the other side of the globe. King George therefore sent a living image, Governor Arthur Philip, vested with the authority of the crown to have dominion over the emerging colony. Such vice-regal appointments bear great privilege and responsibility. The vice-regent is to act on behalf of the king in caring for the dominion of the king in all the complexities of the affairs of the colony.

Image bearing on behalf of the king is at the center of God's purposes for humanity. It is hard to imagine a world in which God delights in his people without also delighting in the place where they live. Commitment to one involves commitment to the other. Indeed, God's commitment to creation is seen throughout Scripture in covenantal terms. Jeremiah proclaims the coming of the new covenant in creational terms. He states:

> Thus says the LORD: If you can break my covenant with the day and my covenant with the night, so that day and night will not come at their appointed time, then also my covenant with David my servant may be broken, so that he shall not have a son to reign on his throne, and my covenant with the Levitical priests my ministers. (Jer. 33:20–21)

Similarly, Jeremiah reminds us of God's covenant with creation as he says: "Thus says the LORD: If I have not established my covenant with day and night and the fixed order of heaven and earth, then I will reject the offspring of Jacob and David my servant" (Jer. 33:25–26). Similar language that talks of a covenant with creation can be found in Hosea 2:18: "And I will make for them a covenant on that day with the beasts of the field, the birds of the heavens, and the creeping things of the ground. And I will abolish the bow, the sword, and war from the land, and I will make you lie down in safety."

In the light of this, it is surprising that so many Christians view the earth as transient at best and something to be forsaken at worst. The opening chapters of Genesis explode this misconception. God's creation is vast, encompassing the expanses of space and the microscopic intricacies of living cells. God's commitment to creation is sure. He will not allow it to be thwarted. Satan will not bring about ultimate destruction through his schemes. God, not Satan, will have the victory over what he has made.

Creation is foundational, but it is not the end of the story; it is the beginning. Within creation God's image bearers reflect the creativity of their Creator. Earth never has been and never will be a static place. It bristles with creativity and development. Animals are named, children are born, poetry is written, and gardens are planted. It is the vibrant home in which we live. And as the Bible spans its story from a garden in Eden to a garden in the new Jerusalem in Revelation 22, we are reminded that God's commitment to his creation does not wane.

The Bible is the story of God's plan to rescue. The scope of that which is fallen is that which will be rescued, restored, and renewed. It is not surprising, therefore, that throughout

Scripture we are told of the fulfillment of this rescue in the words "new heavens and a new earth" (Isa. 65:17; see also 66:22; 2 Pet. 3:13; Rev. 21:1). The teaching about creation is foundational to our understanding of Scripture. The story of the Bible begins at Genesis 1.

2

The Problem with Home

The idyllic beauty of Eden is not a present reality; the presence of evil in this world is a universal fact. Where does evil come from? It's an uneasy question. The mention of Satan, even among Christians, causes confusion or embarrassment. While many people today rail against God's apparent lack of action in the face of evil, only a few people ask the question of evil's origin. Why would an all-powerful and all-loving God allow suffering and injustice? Why does God allow evil to spoil his beautiful world?

Marred Beauty

The Scriptures remind us that God is not inactive in the face of evil, but his solution is to deal not only with the symptoms but also with the cause. The Bible is unambiguous in its assertion that beyond this world there is cosmic opposition to the good purposes of God. Satan is described as a murderer from the beginning who does not stand for the truth (John 8:44); those who succumb to his lies experience murderous consequences. Nothing has changed since Eden. We live in a world where

people make morally wrong decisions with devastating consequences. Yet many continue to scoff at the idea of Satan as they
relativize the concept of evil. Some, however, repent and turn
to Christ for forgiveness. They become a new creation (2 Cor.
5:17) in whom God is at work to bring life in all its abundance
(John 10:10).

Everything changed with the entrance of sin into God's world.
The intimacy between God and his image bearers was marred.
No longer did the Lord God walk with Adam and Eve in the
garden of Eden as had happened previously (Gen. 3:8). Intimacy
between human relationships was replaced by blame between
Adam and Eve and murder between their children. No longer
were they naked and unashamed. Covering up became a way of
life. Intimacy between God's image bearers and the created order
was polluted as even the ground was cursed. God was in control
of his world, but there was now a distance between heaven and
earth. Heaven became a high and holy place separated from the
sin of earth. Heaven is God's space; earth is our space. Heaven
is a place where God's will is done; earth is a place where God's
will is not done as it is in heaven. What is the solution? The reconciliation between heaven and earth that will bring about new
heavens and a new earth will only happen when Satan is removed
from the scene. God promises to crush Satan, the source of the
problem (Gen. 3:15).

This future hope of new heavens and a new earth, of a renewed creation, will happen at God's appointed time. Meanwhile, he continues to wait, "not wishing that any should
perish, but that all should reach repentance" (2 Pet. 3:9). However, his patience should not be confused with inactivity. God's
restorative works are seen every day in anticipation of how it
will be. Through his grace, the effects of sin are addressed. Hurt
results in forgiveness, sickness in healing, hatred in reconcilia-

tion, injustice in mercy, chaos in order—to name a few. God's grace finds greater focus in the proclamation of the gospel. This gospel brings redemption to individual lives and to Christian communities, which results in blessings flowing to marriages, families, friendships, workplaces, and society. God remains concerned for every part of his creation, and the recognition of the lordship of Christ changes everything, everywhere. Amidst the presence of chaos, sickness, and death, God continues to bring life in abundance. And so we pray, "Your will be done, on earth as it is in heaven" (Matt. 6:10), as we await God's final act of restoration.

What do we know about the source of evil? We do not know everything, but we know enough. The Scriptures are sufficient. We know that the origins of sin were beyond Eden. In Genesis 3 we are introduced to an enigmatic talking serpent. He is described in greater detail in the New Testament. He is the devil (Rom. 16:20; cf. Gen. 3:15; Rev. 12:9; 20:2), who appears to be among the fallen heavenly angels referred to in 2 Peter 2:4 and Jude 6. Care should be taken not to read too much back into Genesis. It is important to identify what we know and what we don't know.

We know that evil finds its source in a heavenly yet creaturely rebellion against the Creator. Insofar that the devil is a creature, we know that he will not prevail against the Creator. Insofar as the impact of sin finds its source and effects in the heavens and the earth, its impact will be felt in the relationship between these two realms. The Prodigal Son realized that he had sinned against heaven (Luke 15:21), the repentance of a sinner on earth causes much rejoicing in heaven (Luke 15:7), and a heavenly drama was played out on earth in the book of Job. Earth is never totally independent of the heavenly realms. Indeed, we cannot truly understand the things of earth without an appreciation of the things of heaven, for "we do not wrestle against flesh and blood, but against the rulers, against the authorities, against the cosmic powers over this present darkness, against the spiritual forces of evil in the heavenly places" (Eph. 6:12). Hence the fallout from the entrance of sin into God's good creation is that there is a separation between heaven and earth, and yet this separation is not so exclusive as to eliminate one realm impacting the other.

The Scale of the Tragedy

We are told the *reason* for the fall, the *extent* of the fall, and God's *response* to the fall. Let's turn to each of these. The *reason* for the fall is enunciated by the serpent as he addressed Eve: "You will not surely die. For God knows that when you eat of it your eyes will be opened and you will be like God, knowing good and evil" (Gen. 3:4–5). There is much that can be unpacked from this statement. The serpent sowed doubt in Eve's mind about God's character, but at its core, the temptation revolved around the words: "you will be like God." As Eve and then Adam succumbed to the temptation, they pursued the glory that belongs to God alone. The essence of sin, whether in the heavenly realm or the earthly, is that the creature seeks the glory that belongs to the Creator. The creature should cry with the psalmist:

> Not to us, O Lord, not to us,
>   but to your name give glory. (Ps. 115:1)

But we desire a name for ourselves. Using our God-given talents, we long to glory in our own success. We begin to kid ourselves that we are creating things from nothing. We long to be like God, and we start to believe that we are. The truth is that our talents and abilities find their source in our Creator. When we claim glory for what we have done, we are dealing in stolen goods. It is plagiarism. For the whole of creation exists to bring glory to its Creator.

> The heavens declare the glory of God,
> and the sky above proclaims his handiwork. (Ps. 19:1)

The Westminster Shorter Catechism begins with the well-known question, "What is the chief end of Man?" This is a good question, but it is also restrictive. I wonder if a better question would be, "What is the chief end of creation?" The answer begins, "To glorify God . . ." The reason for sin today is the same as the reason for the original sin in the garden: we long to rob God of his glory as we engage in plagiarism.

If the fall emanates from a desire to be like God and to rob him of his glory, the *extent* of the fall includes all those areas over which humanity has dominion. This includes "the beasts of the field, the birds of the heavens and the fish of the sea" (Ps. 8:7–8). If the vice-regent falls, the effects are felt throughout the whole realm, whether humans, animals, flora, the arts, relational interactions, marine biology—everything. The whole creation is groaning under the weight of the curse of sin as it awaits renewal (Rom. 8:22). God's redemptive purposes address the extent of the effects of the fall. To quote again from Isaac Watts's famous Christmas carol "Joy to the World":

> He comes to make his blessings flow,
> far as the curse is found.[1]

God's Response to the Tragedy

Having seen the *reason* for the fall and its *extent*, we turn our attention to God's *response* to the fall. God's surprising grace

---

1. Isaac Watts, *The Psalms and Hymns of Isaac Watts: With All the Additional Hymns and Complete Indexes*, Great Awakening Writings (Morgan, PA: Soli Deo Gloria, 1997), 173.

is expressed in that he does not obliterate his creation. It would have been reasonable for him to have done so, but he persists with it. He continues with his commitment to creation and sets in process a plan of restoration. That restoration is the focus of this book (and of God's book!). Before tracing that process, we need to ask why he would do that. The answer is found in his covenant with his creation. Let me illustrate this concept before I explain it from Scripture. Any good parent knows about unconditional grace and love. Children do not come with guarantees. From the point of conception, good parents have committed themselves to the child by virtue of the act of procreation. This covenant of procreation will require different things from different parents. For some it will require visits to school principals, to police, and to prisons; for others it will require constantly taking the child to medical appointments; for others it will require the parent to remain committed to the child despite the child wanting nothing to do with the parent. Parenting produces both joy and heartache. Why do we do it? The answer is that good parents remain unconditionally committed to their children because of a covenant of procreation.

The illustration isn't perfect, but it may give a bit of insight into God's commitment to his creation. The very act of creating implies a relationship. When we consider that nothing on this earth exists without God's creative and sustaining purposes, we come to an understanding of his commitment. Not even a sparrow falls to the ground without his knowledge (Matt. 10:29). It is not as though God set everything in motion and then left it to run its own course. Even parenting is not like that! His commitment is ongoing. He sends the rain and the sunshine; he causes the sun to rise and the moon to set.

This covenant with creation is repeatedly referred to in the Old Testament through a specific Hebrew expression, *berith 'olam*, which is translated in our English Bibles as "an everlasting covenant" or sometimes as "a covenant forever." Something is, however, lost in translation from the Hebrew. Whereas it sounds unusual to our English ears to make a covenant with parts of creation that cannot respond (e.g., trees), this highlights a difference in a Hebrew and English understanding of a covenant. We think of a covenant in contractual terms, between two informed, consenting parties. So how can God make a covenant with creation that includes birds, animals, and rocks? It appears preposterous. The Hebrew word *berith*, which means "covenant," can often refer to a one-sided pledge. When God cuts a covenant (*berith*) with Abraham in Genesis 15:18, Abraham is asleep (Gen 15:12). God makes a pledge to Abraham and his descendants. Abraham does respond to God's commands (Gen. 12:4–9; 15:6; 17:22–27), but the covenant is not contingent on human response. Despite the constant faithlessness of Israel in the Old Testament, God remains faithful to his pledge.

The successive covenants in Scripture, whether with Adam, Noah, Abraham, Israel, David, and ultimately the new covenant, find a point of reference in this *everlasting covenant* (*berith 'olam*) made with creation. When God gave Adam the requirement that he not eat of the tree of the knowledge of good and evil (Gen. 2:17), this happened within the context of a preexisting covenant (Hos. 6:7). After the flood, in the days of Noah, we read, "When the bow is in the clouds, I will see it and remember the *everlasting covenant* between God and every living creature of all flesh that is on the earth" (Gen. 9:16). We will see in the next chapter that the Noah narrative describes an act of re-creation that makes sense only in the light of the original creation of all things. Similarly, we see the expression "everlasting covenant" repeatedly used in the Abraham narratives, for example, Genesis 17:7: "I will establish my covenant between me and you and your offspring after you throughout their generations for an *everlasting covenant*, to be God to you and to your offspring after you." We read of the *everlasting covenant* in God's dealings with Moses (Ex. 31:16; Lev. 24:8) and with David (2 Sam. 23:5) and with Israel after the Babylonian exile (Isa. 24:5; 55:3; 61:8; Jer. 32:40; 50:5; Ezek. 16:60; 37:26). In short, God is committed to his creation. The successive covenants he makes find their basis in his prior pledge to all he has made.

The fall is not the beginning of God's purposes of restoration; creation is. We don't start with the problem of sin; we start with the prototype of creation. But neither is the fall the end of the story. The biblical story makes many twists and turns, but God's commitment to creation remains undiminished. God's power over creation is such that even when creation rebels against him, he uses that to which he is opposed to resound to his glory. We see examples of this every day. Healing resounds to God's glory, but it finds its necessary prerequisite in a fruit of the fall: sickness. Forgiveness is at the core of the gospel, but it does not make sense without sin. Even at the point of Jesus's crucifixion, God takes a gross act of injustice, the execution of an innocent man, to demonstrate his righteousness. Satan has done his worst to God's creation, but God remains on his throne and will not allow sin to vanquish his good creation.

What is the Christian to do in this blessed yet cursed world? While we wait and pray for the return of Jesus and the renewal of all things, we do not remain inactive. Creation's glory and the effects of the fall are simultaneously evident in every human endeavor. Christians bring a unique perspective to this. Insofar as we are human, and image bearers together with all people, we join with others in caring for creation (we believe in common grace); insofar as we are Christians and aware of the effects of sin in our world, we seek to be a blessing by bringing a Christian worldview to bear on all that we do. This means that Christians are very aware of the presence and the effects of sin and of the healing power of the Christian gospel. The fall is neither the beginning of the story nor its end, but it is one of the most determinative events within the narrative as we seek to make sense of the world in which we live.

An understanding of the extent of the effects of the fall, and the extent of God's purposes of reclamation, will enable us to see our everyday lives within God's larger narrative. Sickness is a result of the fall, and healing is anticipatory of the new heavens and the new earth; therefore, whether someone works as a nurse, a veterinarian, or a gardener, he or she is not beyond God's commitment to his creation. The same can be said for many pursuits. There are of course some professions or hobbies that are not God-honoring, but many can find their purpose within God's purposes for a fallen world. Christian police officers should understand their vocation as an extension of God's justice; social workers demonstrate God's compassion; artists express God's creativity; farmers show God's commitment to the land. The list goes on. It is the job of the church to equip its members to be salt and light in a fallen world, to demonstrate God's purposes to bless in the light of God's larger narrative. Creation is not thwarted by the fall, but God's commitment to it continues within a world marred by sin. The fall does not cause us to forsake this world but to embrace it with God's justice and grace in the everyday activities of our lives.

3

Cleaning Up Home

One of the earliest accounts of God's commitment to the restoration of creation is seen in the story of Noah and the flood. It is a favorite among children. Animals enter the ark two by two, and children imagine how they were fed and cared for. There is adventure and danger. The story ends with the return of the dove, a promise with a rainbow, and a new beginning for Noah, his family, and the animals. We rejoice that God renews his creational covenant with Noah and his family and with "every living creature that is with [them], the birds, the livestock, and every beast of the earth with [them], as many as came out of the ark; it is for every beast of the earth" (Gen. 9:10).

Cleansing by Water

But that is only one side of the biblical account. The flood is also a story of unparalleled devastation. Never before nor since has there been such widespread destruction. The Bible refers to only two events that involve the destruction of the whole earth: the flood and the second coming of Christ. As such, each of these events helps us to interpret the other. The New Testament describes the final judgment of God upon the world in language that is reminiscent of the flood (e.g., Matt. 24:37; Luke 17:26; 2 Pet. 2:4–10). We will see in this chapter how the second destruction of the world, at the second coming of Christ, is similar to the flood in that it is destruction but not annihilation. The world came through the flood, and it will come through the final judgment. Both events are times of purifying and purging God's creation.

The story of the flood begins with the sons of God desiring the daughters of men and taking them for their wives. This enigmatic union resulted in the birth of the "mighty men who were of old" (Gen. 6:4). The relationship between these inappropriate unions and God's grief over the creation he had made has perplexed biblical scholars for millennia, and I doubt we will solve it here. We know that the sons of God should not have married the daughters of men and produced offspring. But who were they? The problem distils to one question: Were the sons of God human beings or angelic beings? If they were human beings, the passage is probably talking about the marriage between a godly line of Seth (Genesis 5) and an ungodly line of Cain (Gen. 4:17–24). Questions remain. Why would this lead to a flood?

The view that the sons of God were heavenly beings is not without its problems, but it may have a greater claim. The Old Testament calls angels "sons of God" (e.g., Ps. 29:1; Job 1:6; 2:1). Didn't Jesus say that angels neither marry nor are given in marriage (Matt. 22:30; Luke 20:34–36)? However, Genesis 6 is referring to rebellious angels. Can angels perform human functions such as having sexual unions with women? In Genesis angels have human forms as they eat, drink, walk, and talk with people (Gen. 18:1–8; 19:1–3). There is much we don't know. We find it hard to imagine angels having human form, but this may be more to do with our understanding of angels being more spiritual than physical, whereas the Bible sees them as heavenly rather than earthly. In fact, most modern Christians (especially in the West) do not have a well-developed understanding of angels despite the fact that the word *angel* occurs 295 times in the Bible.

Jewish readers of Genesis at the time of the writing of the New Testament did not have such a problem with talking about angels. There had arisen a widely held tradition that the sons of God in Genesis 6 were angels. This idea gained prominence in the period between the close of the Old Testament and the opening of the New, as the intertestamental book *1 Enoch* (ca. second century BC) shows. This book interprets Genesis 6 as referring to a group of fallen angels having union with women, resulting in the creation of a race of destructive creatures whose disembodied spirits lived on after they had slaughtered each other (*1 Enoch* 6–9). This sounds unusual to the modern reader, but its prevalence is seen in the New Testament as evidenced in the book of Jude, which says: "The angels who did not stay within their own position of authority, but left their proper dwelling, he has kept in eternal chains under gloomy darkness until the judgment of the great day—just as Sodom and Gomorrah and the surrounding cities, which likewise indulged in sexual immorality and pursued unnatural desire, serve as an example by undergoing a punishment of eternal fire" (Jude 6–7). It may also be alluded to in 1 Peter 3:19–20, as it relates Christ proclaiming "to the spirits in prison, because they formerly did not obey, when God's patience waited in the days of Noah."

It is important to proceed with appropriate caution in interpreting these very difficult passages. It would appear that the enigmatic passage of Genesis 6:1–4 is understood by the New Testament as talking of improper sexual relations between fallen angelic beings and human women. These inappropriate sexual relations are likened to similar inappropriate sexual relations at Sodom and Gomorrah (2 Pet. 2:5–6; Jude 7). God responds to these acts by judgment that leads to the destruction of the earth, but not to its annihilation.

Many questions remain from this passage. Is the flood a result of "the division" between heaven and earth having been crossed inappropriately? When did these angels fall? Is this interpretation correct? What we do know is that "the wickedness of man was great in the earth, and that every intention of the thoughts of his heart was only evil continually" (Gen. 6:5).

The story of Noah gives us the first mention of the word *covenant* in the Bible. This does not mean that God's covenant with creation was not in existence before the flood. A covenant does not need the use of the word to be a covenant. God's covenant with David in 2 Samuel 7 does not mention the word, although Psalm 89 confirms that it was a covenant (Ps. 89:3). The introduction of the word in the cycle of the Noah stories shows that God is affirming what is already in existence. We see the word repeatedly mentioned (Gen. 6:18; 9:9, 11–13, 15–18). This covenant is not just with Noah but with the whole created order as God now purposes to renew the world through judgment.

The narrative of the flood is, in many senses, a second creation story, and Noah is a second Adam. Both Adam and Noah are made in God's image (Gen. 1:27; 9:6); both are told to be fruitful and multiply and to fill the earth (Gen. 1:28; 9:1, 7). The covenant with Noah is not just a repetition of the original covenant with creation. There has been development. In the light of death having entered the world, animals are to be food for Noah and his family (Gen. 9:3), and there is a prohibition concerning murder (Gen. 9:5–6). As with Adam, God again chooses one man that through his family all the world will be blessed. God's covenant with creation undergirds God's covenant with Noah.

The inclusion of the animals in the Noah story reminds us that God's salvific purposes extend more broadly than just to humanity. No fewer than six times in eight verses are we reminded that God's covenant is with creation (Gen. 9:9–17). God says that a rainbow is "the sign of the covenant that I make between me and you and every living creature that is with you . . . the covenant between me and the earth" (Gen. 9:12–13).

Noah is not only a second Adam in the events of re-creation after the flood, but sadly he also emulates his ancestor Adam in sin. After the flood, Noah shows his commitment to agriculture in planting a grapevine for wine making. Is wine a good thing or a bad thing? On the one hand, "wine gladdens life" (Eccles. 10:19), but it can also be argued that its abuse has been a blight on many parts of society, and Noah's family was no exception. Noah is found drunk and naked at the door of his tent trying to sleep off the effects of his drunkenness (Gen. 9:21). The shame of nakedness is reminiscent of Adam and Eve after the fall in the garden of Eden.

The New Testament picks up on the story of the flood in Peter's two epistles as Noah is mentioned twice by name (1 Pet. 3:20; 2 Pet. 2:5). The final destruction of the world through fire is likened to the destruction of the world at the time of the flood. Peter puts it like this:

> Scoffers will come in the last days with scoffing, following their own sinful desires. They will say, "Where is the promise of his coming? For ever since the fathers fell asleep, all things are continuing as they were from the beginning of creation." For they deliberately overlook this fact, that the heavens existed long ago, and the earth was formed out of

water and through water by the word of God, and that by
means of these the world that then existed was deluged with
water and perished. (2 Pet. 3:3–6)

This is clearly a reference to the flood, the only time in history
when the world has been deluged in such a way by water. This
image is then contrasted with fire as Peter continues:

But by the same word the heavens and earth that now exist
are stored up for fire, being kept until the day of judgment
and destruction of the ungodly. (2 Pet. 3:7)

Cleansing by Fire

The Bible thus talks of two total destructions of the earth: the
former at the time of Noah by water; the latter at the time of
Christ's return by fire. Similar comparisons are found in the
Gospels as Jesus compares judgment by water in the days of
Noah and judgment by fire on the final day. He said:

Just as it was in the days of Noah, so will it be in the days
of the Son of Man. They were eating and drinking and mar-
rying and being given in marriage, until the day when Noah
entered the ark, and the flood came and destroyed them all.
Likewise, just as it was in the days of Lot—they were eating
and drinking, buying and selling, planting and building, but
on the day when Lot went out from Sodom, fire and sulphur
rained from heaven and destroyed them all— so will it be on
the day when the Son of Man is revealed. (Luke 17:26–30)

Will this world be obliterated in this future fiery destruction,
or will this destruction be akin to that of Noah's day when
renewal came through judgment? We turn at this point to a
very difficult but important passage to find the answer: 2 Peter
3:10–13. This passage has fueled the belief among many Chris-

tians that the earth will disappear, and we will find a new home (in heaven). The passage reads:

> But the day of the Lord will come like a thief, and then the heavens will pass away with a roar, and the heavenly bodies will be burned up and dissolved, and the earth and the works that are done on it will be exposed. Since all these things are thus to be dissolved, what sort of people ought you to be in lives of holiness and godliness, waiting for and hastening the coming of the day of God, because of which the heavens will be set on fire and dissolved, and the heavenly bodies will melt as they burn! But according to his promise we are waiting for new heavens and a new earth in which righteousness dwells.

We need to pay close attention to this passage.

The first challenge we have is to determine the original Greek version of the text. The ESV translates 2 Peter 3:10 as "the earth and the works that are done on it will be *exposed*," whereas the older King James Bible, working from a slightly different Greek text, renders the verse: "the earth also and the works that are therein shall be *burned up*." Why the difference? Will the world and its works be exposed, or will it "be burned up"? The issue here is not one of translation but of which is the correct underlying Greek text.

This challenge of determining which variant is the original is not confined to the New Testament. Any document that was written and copied by hand prior to the printing press, such as the writings of Chaucer or Cicero, has such variations. Humans make mistakes, and marginal notes, for example, can become part of the text. We do not have any of the original autographs (the actual piece of material upon which the text was written) of the Old Testament or the New Testament. We have only copies, or copies of copies, that were carefully and reverently reproduced.

At first this may cause some level of disquiet about the authority of our Bibles. In a strange way, however, the variations in the original languages of the Bible should fill us with confidence. We can be grateful that at no time in the history of the text did someone prevail in adopting what they believed to be the authoritative text and in destroying all other texts. Only those who are committed to the truth are happy to live with such tensions. We can also be grateful that since the time of the Reformation, all people have been encouraged to read the Bible. With the advent of the printing press, mass production brought Bibles into people's mother tongues. In the centuries since the Reformation, there have been some discoveries of ancient texts and advances in the science of determining which of the variants is the original. We can be grateful that there are only very few places where the different texts raise any theological consequence, but 2 Peter 3:10 is one such place.

Recent scholarship on Greek manuscripts favors "will be found" (*heurethēsetai*) over "will be burned up" (*katakaēsetai*), and this has been picked up by modern translations, in addition to the ESV: "and the earth and everything that is done on it will be disclosed" (NRSV); "and the earth and the works on it will be disclosed" (HCSB); "and the earth and everything done in it will be laid bare" (NIV). But for several hundred years the influence of the King James Bible has been felt as people have read, "the earth also and the works that are therein shall be burned up." This has resulted in a widespread belief in the annihilation both of the world and any work done within it. But as in the days of Noah, so at the coming of Christ—destruction through judgment does not mean annihilation.[1]

1. Al Wolters, "Worldview and Textual Criticism in 2 Peter 3:10," *Westminster Theological Journal* 49 (1987): 405–13.

The image of 2 Peter 3 is that of a purifying fire such as is used to purify gold. The process of purification does not result in the destruction of the gold; the dross is removed, and the purity of the gold is found. A similar image is found in 1 Corinthians 3:12–15:

> Now if anyone builds on the foundation with gold, silver, precious stones, wood, hay, straw—each one's work will become manifest, for the Day will disclose it, because it will be revealed by fire, and the fire will test what sort of work each one has done. If the work that anyone has built on the foundation survives, he will receive a reward. If anyone's work is burned up, he will suffer loss, though he himself will be saved, but only as through fire.

The end result of the purging will be the total transformation that brings in "new heavens and a new earth in which righteousness dwells" (2 Pet. 3:13). It is hard to conceive of what a sinless world will look like, but it will be simultaneously this world and yet totally transformed as through fire. Not only will the world be purified as through fire, but the works that are done in it will be exposed for what they really are. Human achievements will be purged of their dross, and what is pure will remain.

The two biblical accounts of worldwide destruction are not examples of God's rejection of the world and of the futility of works done in the world. They are reminders of God's commitment to the earth, which includes works done in it. This earth will be purged. Our eternal home will be a renewed earth. God's commitment to this earth has not waned since Eden. His commitment to all he has made leads to cleansing—whether by water or by fire. What we do here matters to him.

4

A Place God Calls Home

Christians often feel like third-culture kids, those who live in a country or culture that is different from that of their parents. They speak one language at home and another at school. When asked where home is, the answer is probably somewhere in an airport. They live between worlds and have a sense of not belonging. Where do Christians belong? If our home is really earth, doesn't that make us third-culture kids, with our Father being in heaven? In the light of this, it is helpful to develop the biblical theme of God's *earthly* home: the temple.

God's Home on Earth

The first temple we see in the Bible is the garden of Eden. In the context of the ancient Near East, a temple was a place where the deity met with his people. It was a microcosm of everything over which the god ruled. The temple of the Babylonian god Marduk was a "counterpart of what he brought to pass in heaven."[1] Similar understandings of temples as a reflection

1. G. K. Beale, *The Temple and the Church's Mission: A Biblical Theology of the Dwelling Place of God* (Downers Grove, IL: InterVarsity Press, 2004), 51.

of heaven can be found among Egyptian, Mesopotamian, and Sumerian civilizations.[2] Eden was also a microcosm of the universe over which God ruled, but with a difference. Whereas other temples had images of deities made of wood and stone, the image bearers in Eden were living human beings named Adam and Eve (Gen. 1:27). Whereas other temples were lifeless buildings, Eden was a growing and developing garden.

Within God's Edenic temple we find a priest named Adam who met with God in this garden (Gen. 3:8). We read: "The LORD God took the man and put him in the garden of Eden to *work* it and *keep* it" (Gen. 2:15). The Hebrew words translated "work" and "keep" (*'abad* and *shamar*) are found throughout the Old Testament for service in the temple, where they are translated "serve" and "keep" (e.g., Num. 3:7–8; 8:25–26; 18:5–6; 1 Chron. 23:32; Ezek. 44:14).[3] Unfortunately, Adam failed to guard the garden/temple from the intrusion of the serpent, and so his work/service within it was compromised.

This garden imagery of God's earthly dwelling continued in the tabernacle that Moses was instructed to build (Exodus 25–31) and in the more permanent temple built by Solomon in Jerusalem (1 Kings 6). Garden imagery such as pomegranates was depicted on the priests' garments in the tabernacle (Ex. 28:33–34; 39:24–26) and in the temple (1 Kings 7:18, 20, 42). Palm trees and open flowers were carved onto walls and doors of the temple (1 Kings 6:29, 32, 35). Cherubim were woven into the curtain that formed the tabernacle's outer wall (Ex. 26:1, 31; 36:8, 35), a reminder of the cherubim who guarded the way to the tree of life in the garden of Eden after Adam and Eve were banished from it (Gen. 3:24). Cherubim also guarded the lid of the ark of the covenant, both in the tabernacle (Ex.

---

2. Ibid., 51–52.
3. Ibid., 67.

25:18–20; 37:7–9) and in the temple (1 Kings 6:23–38; 8:6–7). As the priest ventured toward the holiest part of the tabernacle/ temple, he would pass a lampstand with seven branches (Ex. 25:33–36), which may have resembled the tree of life in the middle of the garden. The priest was dressed in a blue robe bejeweled with precious stones that reminded him of the blue-black night and the stars of space and pomegranates of the garden (Ex. 28:31–37; 39:31). The precious stones in the temple were the same as those in Eden: gold, bdellium, and onyx (Gen. 2:12; cf. Ex. 25:7, 11–39; 1 Kings 6:20–22; 1 Chron. 29:2). In so many ways, the tabernacle and the temple were a reminder of God's commitment to the world he had created.

This link between Eden and the tabernacle is not insignificant. Within the context of Adam's priestly failure, a corporate Adam, Israel, was given the role of dominion over the earth. Israel would act as God's vice-regent, a role that had belonged to Adam. Israel would represent God on earth as a kingdom of priests (Ex. 19:6). God would dwell with Israel in the tabernacle, which is likened to a royal palace made of materials such as gold, silver, bronze, different types of leather, acacia wood, oil, spices and incense, and onyx stones (Ex. 25:3–7). This new beginning, of a new Adam, Israel, happens in the context of traveling from Egypt to a new Eden, the Promised Land.

The exodus narrative is not just a story about getting from Egypt to Israel. If that were the case, it could have happened far more efficiently. It is only 462 miles (743 kilometers) from Cairo to Jerusalem. Walking with a large group of elderly people, children, pregnant women, and the infirm would have its challenges, but even if such a group could do 12 to 16 miles (20–25 kilometers) a day, six days a week, it would take around forty days—which is a lot quicker than forty years! But this journey is not just about the destination. God is doing a new thing on the journey as he forms this corporate Adam called Israel, his firstborn son (Ex. 4:22), whom he will put in a new garden, the Promised Land. God has not forgotten his covenant with creation (Hos. 2:18), with Noah (Gen. 6:18; 9:9–18), or with Abraham (Gen 18:18; 22:18) to bless all the nations of the earth. God is traveling with his people in the tabernacle.

The requirement that was placed on Israel in the Promised Land is similar to that which was placed on Adam in the garden of Eden: obedience. The Ten Commandments, the requirements of obedience, are reiterated upon entry to the land (Deut. 5:7–21). Obedience will lead to blessing; disobedience to curse (Deut. 30:19, 20). This struggle between obedience and disobedience, between blessing and curse, continues throughout the Old Testament. At a general level, God's covenant with creation continues: the sun rises, the rain falls, and the seasons change. But at a more particular level, the role of corporate Adam (Israel) to bring the blessing of redemption and restoration to creation is contingent upon obedience. To this end, God in his grace provides for disobedience in his house, the tabernacle. Once a year, on the Day of Atonement, sacrifices are made for the sins of the nation (Lev. 16:1–34).

Several hundred years after the Israelites arrived in the land, the first temple was built. Its construction came in the context of a golden age when Israel had peace from warfare (2 Sam. 7:1). The land was truly conquered. David, the greatest of the Israelite kings, was on the throne and living in luxury (2 Sam. 5:11; 7:2) while the house of God was still a tent (2 Sam. 6:17). David resolved to build God's house. But King David needed to learn an important lesson. It's not about him doing things for God; it's about God doing things through him. God had granted the victories, given the land, and kept his covenant.

It all begins and ends with God. God's reply to the prophet Nathan is instructive:

> Go and tell my servant David, "Thus says the LORD: Would you build me a house to dwell in? I have not lived in a house since the day I brought up the people of Israel from Egypt to this day, but I have been moving about in a tent for my dwelling. In all places where I have moved with all the people of Israel, did I speak a word with any of the judges of Israel, whom I commanded to shepherd my people Israel, saying, 'Why have you not built me a house of cedar?'" (2 Sam. 7:5–7)

God was to be the architect of the temple. God is always the author of his own worship. His house would be built at his time according to his initiative.

The temple was built by David's son, Solomon, on Mount Moriah (2 Chron. 3:1) as a reminder that it was there that God had provided a substitutionary sacrifice for Isaac (Gen. 22:2) through the provision of a ram in the thicket (Gen. 22:13). As with the tabernacle, the instructions for building the temple came from God himself (Ex. 25:9, 40; 1 Chron. 28:19). Although no house can contain God (1 Kings 8:27; 2 Chron. 2:6; 6:18), upon the completion of the temple, the glory cloud filled the temple (1 Kings 8:10–13; 2 Chron. 5:13–6:2) as had also been the case in the tabernacle (Ex. 33:9; 40:35; Num. 9:15–16; 16:42). This was God's house. His presence distinguished the temple from all other buildings. Similarly, God's presence in the temple distinguished Israel from all the other nations. Israel was the new corporate Adam. Therefore, when the temple was destroyed in 586 BC by Nebuchadnezzar's armies (Jer. 52:12–23) and its treasure taken into exile (Ezra 5:14; 6:5), this was both a national and a theological disaster. Israel awaited God's presence to return and for the temple to be rebuilt. God's presence on earth is a central theme in Scripture.

When we come to the New Testament, we read that Jesus is the new temple. As the Gospel of John opens, we read: "the Word became flesh and dwelt among us" (John 1:14). The word translated "dwelt" in the original Greek literally means "tabernacled." God now dwells with his corporate Adam on earth as had been the case in the garden, in the wilderness wanderings, and in Jerusalem. John 1:51 shows that in Jesus, heaven and earth are reunited. Jesus states, "Truly, truly, I say to you, you will see heaven opened, and the angels of God ascending and descending on the Son of Man." This is a clear allusion to Jacob's dream at Bethel of a "ladder set on the earth, and the top of it reached to heaven" (Gen. 28:12). When Jacob awoke he exclaimed, "This is none other than the house of God, and this is the gate of heaven" (Gen. 28:16–17). Jesus explains that his death and resurrection will fulfill the temple. He said: "Destroy this temple, and in three days I will raise it up" (John 2:19). John gives us editorial comment that Jesus "was speaking about the temple of his body. When therefore he was raised from the dead, his disciples remembered that he had said this, and they believed the Scripture and the word that Jesus had spoken" (John 2:21–22).

The Father's House

In the light of the repeated temple imagery in the Fourth Gospel, it is surprising that when we come to Jesus's reference to his Father's house in John 14:1–6, it is often read as heaven and not as the temple. Jesus states: "In my Father's house are many rooms. If it were not so, would I have told you that I go to prepare a place for you? And if I go and prepare a place for you, I will come again and will take you to myself, that where I am you may be also" (John 14:2, 3). The passage is often preached at funerals. The sermon goes a bit like this: the deceased was someone who trusted in Jesus, and therefore we do not need to be troubled because he or she has gone home to the Father's house in heaven. There is then a plea for people to turn to Jesus in the light of their own impending death, for Jesus says: "I am the way, and the truth, and the life. No one comes to the Father except through me" (John 14:6).

There is much truth in this sermon. It talks about the exclusivity of Jesus for salvation, about our hope in the face of death, about the reality of heaven. But are we missing something in this passage? John 14 is not primarily about the death of the believer; it is about the death of Jesus. Jesus had just washed the disciples' feet (John 13:1–20), and he was about to go to the cross. In this context, Jesus comforted the disciples with the knowledge that he will come again (John 14:3). The Bible knows nothing of Jesus returning to earth every time Christians die, to take them to heaven, as is implied by this oft-preached funeral sermon! Furthermore, at the time of Jesus, it would be unlikely that his original audience would have understood the expression "my Father's house" (John 14:2) to refer to heaven; it would have been heard as a reference to the temple, which dominated the skyline of Jerusalem. The only other occurrence of the same expression in John's Gospel is when Jesus said, "Do not make my Father's house a house of trade" (John 2:16).

John 14 is set in the context of Jesus speaking about his impending death. Jesus informed the disciples that he would be with them for only a little while longer (John 13:33) at which Peter remonstrates: "Lord, why can I not follow you now? I will lay down my life for you" (John 13:37). This sets the scene for the opening of John 14 where Jesus tenderly said to his disciples, "Let not your hearts be troubled" (John 14:1), and proceeded to talk about going to "my Father's house" (John 14:2). This is a reference to the cross. The Father's house, the temple, is fulfilled in the cross. The cross is the fulfillment of all that the temple stood for. It was the place of sacrifice where heaven and earth would meet. It would be through the cross and resurrection that God would dwell with his people. The cross was where Jesus was going, and this was the reason for Peter's concern.

At this point we need to do a bit of detailed work to make sense of this passage. The translation of John 14:2 is normally rendered, "In my Father's house are many rooms." As far as translations go, this is okay, but, as we know, something is always lost in translation, and that is certainly the case here. The word translated "rooms" is *monai* (singular *monē*), which comes from the Greek word *menō*, which means "to abide" or "to remain." This word is prominent in the next chapter of John, when Jesus refers to himself as the true vine in whom we are to abide/remain (John 15:4–10, 16). Jesus is therefore saying that within God's house (the temple, here fulfilled in the cross) are many rooms in which his disciples can abide/remain. What sort of room is this?

It is interesting to note how John 14:2 has been translated over the years. In a strange way, older translations may help us. The King James Version (1611) of John 14:2 begins: "In My Father's house are many mansions." This sounds unusual to the modern ear. How can you have a mansion inside a house? A similar expression is found in the Tyndale Bible (1523), which says: "In my fathers housse [*sic*] are many mansions." The word *mansion* has changed its meaning in the last five hundred years. In the late Middle Ages, it meant a place at which to halt along the way.[4] How will God abide with his people after the

---

4. This is what the word *mansio* means in Latin: "Night-quarters, lodging-place, inn." *A Latin Dictionary founded on Andrews' Edition of Freund's Latin Dictionary*, ed. C.T. Lewis and C. Short (Oxford, UK: Clarendon, 1879), s.v. *mansio*. Jerome used this

cross, when he comes again three days later at the resurrection? How will he continue to abide with us as we travel on the way in the Christian life? The answer is through the gift of the Spirit. Later in John 14 we see another occurrence of the same Greek word (*monē*) in the context of Jesus's promises concerning the coming of the Holy Spirit. Jesus says, "We will come to him and make our *home* [*monē*] with him" (John 14:23).

So why is Jesus telling Peter not to be troubled, in the light of Jesus's coming death (John 14:1)? Jesus will come again. This is not a reference to the believer's death, but to the resurrection and the consequent gift of the Spirit. God is not leaving them (or us). He will abide with us by the Spirit. He will abide with us as we await our final home at the second coming of Jesus. He will not leave the disciples (or us) as orphans (John 14:18). The Spirit will continue the temple function of God abiding with us.

At this point, we need to look at another issue of translation. In John 14:3 we read, "I will come again and will *take* you to myself." This sounds like Jesus will take us elsewhere, but in Greek the original word (*paralambanō*) can mean either "take" or "receive." Most translators have used "take" on the assumption that Jesus is talking about taking believers to heaven. But if our interpretation is correct, it would be better to translate the verse, "I will come again and will *receive* you to myself, that where I am you may be also."

Jesus revealed an amazing truth in John 14. In the Old Testament, God had dwelt in his house at only one place at a time, whether in Eden or in the tabernacle or in the temple in Jerusalem. This is even the case in the time of the earthly life of Jesus. After the resurrection, God will dwell with his people

word in his Latin translation (AD 405): "in domo Patris mei mansiones multæ sunt." *The Vulgate New Testament with The Douay Version of 1582 in Parallel Columns* (London: Samuel Bagster & Sons, 1872), 146. This Latin use influenced the use of "mansions" in the English.

wherever they are. The Spirit replaces geographical limitations as God dwells with his people. In John 14:1–6 Jesus was giving a picture not of going home to heaven but of going to the cross from which he will come again at the resurrection and in the gift of the Spirit. All this, however, hinges on Jesus going to the Father's house, his death and resurrection, where heaven and earth meet, where substitutionary atonement is made. This is the temple *par excellence*. Jesus is the way, the truth, and the life.

5

The Land as Home

An appreciation of land is more than an understanding of dirt. In the modern Western world, the concept of land has been reduced to a commodity we call "real estate." Many societies have a more multifaceted understanding of land. The traditional belief among Australian Aborigines is that we do not own land; it owns us. The land gave birth to us, feeds us, and at death will receive us back. There is a level of truth to this, although it can also lead to pantheism in which creation and not the Creator is worshiped. When European explorers raced to Australia to claim the land for their distant king, it created a clash of worldviews that is still not resolved.

The Promised Land

Land is where we belong. It is a place of heritage and identity. Agricultural communities understand this. The farm is not owned by anyone; it is held in trust from one generation to the next. A couple of years ago I was in Yorkshire in England, from where my grandfather emigrated to Australia. I have never lived there, and their regional accent is nearly incomprehensible to my ears. But in a strange way I felt that I belonged. My ancestors lived there for centuries.

There is a growing interest in tracing our ancestry as a quest for identity and belonging. Questions abound around belonging. Who owns Kashmir? Tibet? The Balkans? What is the solution to land disputes between Israelis and Palestinians? These are not just issues about dirt and real estate.

In the light of our inclination to see land as a commodity, it is not surprising that many of us fail to have a robust theology of the land. This is a pity, as God's intentions for one land, Israel, have ramifications for the future of the whole earth. It is instructive that both in Hebrew and in Greek (the languages of the two Testaments of the Bible), the same word can be used for dirt, for one specific land, or for the whole earth. In Hebrew the word 'erets is used to refer to the entire earth (e.g., Gen. 1:1; 11:1), to land in general (Ex. 8:22), or to the land occupied by a nation such as Moab (Deut. 1:5). In the Greek New Testament, the word for land is gē, which, like 'erets, can also refer to the whole earth (Rev. 3:10), to a political area such as the land of Judah (Matt. 2:6), or to soil (Mark 4:8).

Land is integral to our existence. We often talk about how the gospel redeems people, without thinking about where those people will live. We know that human beings need a physical world in which to survive. Without air, food, and water we perish. But if we believe in a physical resurrection (which is clearly the teaching of the Bible), will not those renewed bodies also need a renewed world in which to live? What will that world look like? It is at this point that we need an expanded vision of what God is doing in his world. For many, an articulation of the gospel is, "If I believe in Jesus, I will live with him forever." That is true but reductionistic. The gospel is not just about *my* salvation. Jesus's resurrection impacts everything, including a renewed earth upon which our resurrected bodies will live.

Questions abound about this renewal of the earth. The apostle John reminds us: "What we will be has not yet appeared; but we know that when he appears we shall be like him, because we shall see him as he is" (1 John 3:2). But this does not mean we are totally ignorant. Much has already been revealed. We know that land is more than a commodity and less than a god. It is to be neither exploited nor worshiped. As part of the created order, it is a prominent character in the biblical narrative. It nourishes (Lev. 26:4), devours its inhabitants (Num. 13:32), and mourns (Jer. 23:10). It can be remembered (Lev. 26:42), abandoned (Lev. 26:43), defiled (Lev. 18:25, 27; Deut. 21:23), cleansed (Deut. 32:43), subdued (Josh. 18:10), cursed (Deut. 29:27; Jer. 44:22), and polluted (Jer. 3:1). It even observes the Sabbath (Lev. 25:2). Its story begins with the opening of the Bible (Gen. 1:1) and finds its consummation at the end (Rev. 21:1). What happens in between is determined by these bookends. We are never independent of land.

Within this understanding of God's ownership of the entire earth, we are introduced to the concept of a Holy Land. This concept begins in Eden, where God's presence sanctifies the land (Gen. 3:8). The theme continues as Moses is instructed to remove his sandals because he is standing on holy ground (Ex. 3:5). It is God's presence that sanctifies the land. During the exile to Babylon, God is still present with his people. The question of Ezekiel 1 is whether God dwells with his people even though they are outside the land of Israel. The answer comes in the form of a vision of the chariot throne of the Lord traveling east from Jerusalem and appearing on the banks of the Chebar River in Babylon (Ezek. 1:1–28). God's presence is not confined to the borders of Israel.

The choosing of a particular land in which God's presence would dwell is found in God's promise to Abraham. Although land is not specifically mentioned in Genesis 12:1–3, it is made more specific in the repetition of the promise in Genesis 15: "On that day the LORD made a covenant with Abram, saying, 'To your offspring I give this land, from the river of Egypt to the great river, the river Euphrates'" (Gen. 15:18). It is likely that "the river of Egypt" is not the Nile but the Wadi el-Arish in the northeastern Sinai, which is referred to in the Old Testament as the "Brook of Egypt" (Num. 34:5; Josh. 15:4, 47; 1 Kings 8:65; 2 Kings 24:7; 2 Chron. 7:8; Isa. 27:12; Ezek. 47:19; 48:29). This river is situated about 17 miles (27 kilometers) south of the modern Israeli-Egyptian border. The borders of Israel have reached this southern extreme (Josh. 15:47; 1 Kings 8:65; 2 Chron. 7:8; cf. Ezek. 47:19; 48:24). Similarly, the land of Israel has also reached the northern reaches of the Euphrates River (Deut. 11:24; 2 Sam. 8:3; 1 Kings 4:24; 1 Chron. 18:3). At the peak of Israel's territorial expansions, the Bible says of King Solomon: "He ruled over all the kings from the Euphrates to the land of the Philistines and to the border of Egypt" (2 Chron. 9:26). These borders are referred to as "Greater Israel" among modern Zionist debates. Israel's borders are more specifically defined in Numbers 34:2–12, which is later confirmed when Joshua leads the Israelites into the land (Josh. 5:10–12). Disputes continue into the current day, but the boundaries of biblical Israel (not Greater Israel) are normally seen as from the Mediterranean in the west, to the Jordan in the east (and possibly some area beyond the Jordan), to Dan in the north and Beersheba in the south (Judg. 20:1).

The Promised Land is described in superlative terms. To the exodus generation, it is described as flowing with milk and honey (Ex. 3:8, 17; 13:5; 33:3). It is often compared to Eden.

Even though there were inhabitants in the land prior to its conquest under Joshua, this reentry to the land is seen at one level as an act of re-creation.[1] As with creation, the formation of the land culminates in sabbath when Israel has rest from her enemies (e.g., 2 Sam. 7:1; 1 Kings 4:25; 8:56; cf. Pss. 95:11; 132:13–14). The land is placed under God's vice-regent David, who is a man after God's own heart (1 Sam. 13:14; Acts 13:22). As with God's covenant with Adam, blessing in the land is contingent upon obedience (Deut. 4:25–27).

The land is to be holy, for it is God's land. The inhabitants of the land are to be holy (Num. 35:34); their disobedience results in the land's defilement (e.g., Lev. 18:26–27; Jer. 2:7). Those who live in the land are but trustees (Lev. 25:23). The land and its produce belong to God (Lev. 27:30–33; Deut. 14:22; 26:9–15). Should the land become defiled through disobedience, it will expel its inhabitants (Lev. 18:24–30; 20:22; Deut. 4:25–27) as happened in the garden of Eden and with the Babylonian captivity.

Return to the land from the Babylonian exile is also likened to the restoration of Eden:

> For the LORD comforts Zion;
> > he comforts all her waste places
> and makes her wilderness like Eden,
> > her desert like the garden of the LORD;
> joy and gladness will be found in her,
> > thanksgiving and the voice of song.
> > (Isa. 51:3; cf. Ezek. 36:35)

The blessings that flowed from Eden and watered the whole earth will be restored through the reestablishment of exiled

---

1. Munther Isaac, *From Land to Lands, from Eden to the Renewed Earth* (Carlisle, UK: Langham, 2015), 154n1. See also Christopher J. H. Wright, *Old Testament Ethics for the People of God* (Leicester, UK: Inter-Varsity Press, 2004), 137–44.

Israel in this Edenic land. But how and when does this happen? The answer is found in the forgiveness of the defilement that led to exile, in the obedience that is required for blessing, and in a re-creation of land that leads to blessings flowing to the whole earth. We see the fulfillment of all these requirements in the ministry of Israel's messiah, Jesus the Christ.

From the Land to the Earth

How does the New Testament continue the Bible's teaching about land? It would be an understatement to say that there is a level of confusion on this topic. At one extreme there are those who see a continuation of God's purposes for Israel being fulfilled in the modern state of Israel, recognized by the United Nations in 1948 and extended in bloody conflicts in ensuing wars. At the other extreme, there are those who hold that the New Testament does not address the issue of land but sees the fulfillment of an understanding of the land in nonterrestrial terms. Neither of these views is held by this author. As with all Old Testament promises, the promises concerning land find their fulfillment in the ministry of Jesus, the Christ (2 Cor. 1:20). What does such fulfillment result in? The answer is clear from the Old Testament. Fulfillment leads to God's blessings filling the entire earth. No longer do we need to talk of a holy land, but we can now talk of a holy earth, filled with the glory of God through the gift of his Spirit. God's presence makes the whole earth holy. The earth is not to be worshiped, but creation care is an important Christian activity.

The fulfillment of an Old Testament understanding of the land is not seen in the continuation of a political state called Israel. As the New Testament opens, each of the Gospels mentions a man by the name of John, who is performing a baptism of repentance in the wilderness of Judea (Matt. 3:1; Mark 1:4;

Luke 3:3; John 1:26). This baptism should be seen not merely in individualistic terms. It is a baptism of judgment upon the disobedience of Israel and her leaders. They are addressed as a "brood of vipers" (Matt. 3:7; Luke 3:7). Judgment upon Israel is seen in images such as a baptism of fire (Matt. 3:11), an ax at the root of the tree (Matt. 3:10; Luke 3:9), and a winnowing fork placing chaff into an unquenchable fire (Matt. 3:12; Luke 3:17). Israel's disobedience has led to judgment. John announces the end of the nation of Israel being seen as a holy people living in a holy land.

Amidst the judgment upon Israel caused by disobedience appears one who will bring blessing through obedience. Jesus appears as Israel's Messiah. Messiahs are those anointed to act on behalf of those they represent. When David fought Goliath (1 Samuel 17), both men were messiahs acting on behalf of their people. When David won the battle, so did Israel; when Goliath lost, so did the Philistines. The hopes of the respective nations were realized in their messiahs. Jesus is the Messiah who acts on behalf of his people, Israel. He was anointed for this role in the baptism of John, and a voice was heard from heaven declaring him to be God's son (Matt. 3:17; Mark 1:11; Luke 3:22), as both Adam (Luke 3:38) and Israel (Ex. 4:22) are described. Jesus fulfilled the roles of Israel. But unlike Adam and Israel before him, Jesus would prove to be the obedient son of God. Jesus underwent the baptism of repentance for the sins of Israel (Matt. 3:16; Mark 1:9; Luke 3:21). This baptism in the Jordan for the forgiveness of sins prefigures a greater baptism: Jesus's death upon the cross (Luke 12:50). Israel is reborn through the forgiveness of her sins found in her Messiah, who acts on her behalf. The firstfruits of this rebirth are seen three days after the messiah's death, when he rose from the grave. Jesus is not just the vine that typified Israel in the Old Testament (Ps. 80:8,

14; Isa. 5:1–7; Hos. 10:1); he is the *true* vine (John 15:1). The boundaries of Israel are no longer drawn on a map but around Jesus. In Jesus, God's plan to bless the earth will be fulfilled.

The New Testament then becomes the story of how the promises to the people of Israel are fulfilled in the obedience of her Messiah. The covenanted blessings to Adam and to Israel flow to the Gentiles and to the ends of the earth. Since the time of John the Baptist, the true Israel is to be understood as those who are united with Israel's Messiah, Jesus, regardless of whether they be Jew or Gentile, male or female, slave or free (Gal. 3:28). But this doesn't mean that God has given up on the earth and that we are to understand Israel in purely spiritual categories. When the sin of Israel's disobedience is forgiven, the door is reopened to Eden. On the cross, Jesus proclaimed to the penitent thief: "Today you will be with me in paradise" (Luke 23:43). The word *paradise* is the same word that is used of Eden in the Greek translation of Genesis 2 and 3 (Gen. 2:8–9, 15; 3:1–3, 8, 10, 23–24). The door to Eden, which since the fall has been blocked, is being reopened by Jesus's sacrificial death. The groaning of all creation, awaiting its liberation, will find its healing because of the ministry of Jesus (Rom. 8:19–23).

God has not given up on this world. Our resurrected bodies will live in a renewed earth. God's presence will fill all, as indeed is already happening in the gift of the Holy Spirit, who dwells with us on earth. He is the guarantee of what will happen (2 Cor. 5:5; Eph. 1:14). We do not cry, "I cannot wait to leave this world." We certainly do not look at a purely spiritualized fulfillment of Israel. Israel will be fulfilled in the renewal of the earth. It is a good exercise to stare out the window from time to time and to contemplate how interdependent we are with the earth in which we live. We care for it as it cares for us. Yet in so many ways, there is so much wrong with this world.

Modern conservationists remind us that there is no planet B. They are correct. But God intends to fix up planet A. We are to care for it, but we are powerless to effect a total renewal of it. So we cry, "Maranatha," which means "Our Lord, come!" (1 Cor. 16:22). "Come, Lord Jesus!" (Rev. 22:20).

6

The Promise of a Better Home

One of our challenges in reading the New Testament is knowing what has preceded it. We may know some Old Testament stories about Noah, Abraham, Moses, and David, but when we come to the second half of the Old Testament, our familiarity starts to wane. Prophets proclaim judgment. There is an exile to Babylon and a return to Judea. What has this got to do with the New Testament? The answer is, much more than we may have at first appreciated.

Return from Exile

As soon as we open the New Testament, we note that God's people are coming home from exile. Matthew's Gospel begins with a genealogy that is divided into three neat sections, each consisting of fourteen generations: from Abraham to David, from David to the Babylonian deportation, and from this deportation to Christ (Matt. 1:1–17). Why is the Babylonian exile given such prominence?

In the Old Testament there are three major exiles: from the garden of Eden, from Egypt, and to Babylon. The return from these exiles helps us to understand the ministry of Jesus. The exodus from Egypt is celebrated annually in the Passover festival, when Jewish people remember their salvation from the tenth plague during which the blood of a lamb was placed on the door lintels of Jewish homes in Egypt and how the angel of death passed over those houses. The Passover meal retells the story through cups of wine. During one such meal, Jesus takes one of these cups and says, "This cup that is poured out for you is the new covenant in my blood" (Luke 22:20). A new Israel now has a new covenant, which is established by a new defining story: a new exodus sealed by the blood of the Messiah. Jesus will bring the people of God home from the Babylonian exile.

This raises an obvious question. Hadn't the Israelites already returned from the Babylonian exile over five hundred years before Jesus's birth? The answer depends on what we are asking. If we are asking whether they were back in the land, the answer is clearly yes. If we are asking whether God had returned to dwell with his people in the land, we get a different answer. After the Babylonian exile, the temple was rebuilt, but there is no record of the Lord filling this rebuilt temple, as had been the case with the first temple (1 Kings 8:10–13; 2 Chron. 5:13–6:2). If God did not live in his earthly home, were they truly home? Jeremiah had foretold that the return from the Babylonian exile would mark the beginning of a new Israel in a way similar to how the return from the Egyptian exile had established the old Israel. He prophesied:

> Therefore, behold, the days are coming, declares the LORD, when they shall no longer say, "As the LORD lives who brought up the people of Israel out of the land of Egypt," but "As the LORD lives who brought up and led the off-

spring of the house of Israel out of the north country and out of all the countries where he had driven them." Then they shall dwell in their own land. (Jer. 23:7–8)

This return from exile happens in the ministry of Jesus.

Matthew continues the theme of return from the Babylonian exile, after the opening genealogy. Similarities are drawn between Moses and Joshua, who led the Israelites home from Egypt, and Jesus, who leads his people home from Babylon. An angel appears to Joseph and tells him to name Mary's son Jesus, the Greek form of the Hebrew name Joshua. Joseph, Mary, and Jesus flee from Herod's pogrom in Bethlehem to Egypt, and on their return Matthew cites, "Out of Egypt I called my son" (Matt. 2:15; cf. Hos. 11:1). Jesus reenters the land of Judea by crossing the Jordan in his baptism (Matt. 3:13–16), which reminds us of how his namesake also crossed the same river (Josh. 3:17). Jesus is declared to be God's Son (Matt. 3:17), as was Israel (Ex. 4:22). Jesus does not succumb to temptation when he is tempted in the wilderness for forty days (Matt. 4:1–11), unlike Israel, whose disobedience for forty days led to forty years of wilderness wanderings (Num. 14:33–34). Israel was given the law at Mount Sinai (Ex. 20:1–17); Jesus teaches even greater obedience to this law in the sermon on another mount (Matthew 5–7). Jesus is the new and greater Moses (Deut. 18:15–18), who brings his people back from the Babylonian exile in an even greater way than Moses and Joshua brought the people back from the Egyptian exile.

An appreciation of the theological and historical contexts of this return from the Babylonian exile will help us to better understand Jesus's ministry. We will begin by looking at the theological context in this chapter, and in the next chapter we will address the historical context. This theological context is found in the major prophets of the Old Testament. We now turn our attention to three of these: Isaiah, Jeremiah, and Ezekiel.

Isaiah

Isaiah lived in the eighth century BC, prior to the exile. The book that bears his name begins in Jerusalem, where the prophet is given a message of doom and destruction. He receives this message through one of the most majestic pictures of God dwelling in the temple. Whereas earlier descriptions of the temple were of perceptible realities—acacia wood, precious metals, and courts—in Isaiah 6:1–4, Isaiah sees the imperceptible realities within the court of heaven. Six-winged seraphs hover above the divine throne crying, "Holy, holy, holy" (Isa. 6:3), as Isaiah is given a message of coming exile and subsequent return. He is also told that his proclamation will fall on deaf ears! God instructs Isaiah to say to the people:

> "Keep on hearing, but do not understand;
>   keep on seeing, but do not perceive."
> Make the heart of this people dull,
>   and their ears heavy,
>   and blind their eyes;
> lest they see with their eyes,
>   and hear with their ears,
> and understand with their hearts,
>   and turn and be healed. (Isa. 6:9–10)

This would not be easy! The message of exile and return is described in agricultural terminology of uprooting and replanting:

> Then I said, "How long, O Lord?"
> And he said:
> "Until cities lie waste
>   without inhabitant,

and houses without people,
>   and the land is a desolate waste,
and the LORD removes people far away,
>   and the forsaken places are many in the midst of the
>   land.
And though a tenth remain in it,
>   it will be burned again,
like a terebinth or an oak,
>   whose stump remains
>   when it is felled."
The holy seed is its stump. (Isa. 6:11–13)

Isaiah's commission helps us to see how Jesus's ministry is presented as a return from exile. Jesus told several parables about planting seeds, but the best known is about a sower who sowed seed on four different kinds of soil: a path, rocky soil, thorny soil, and good soil (Matt. 13:3–9; Mark 4:1–9; Luke 8:4–8). In the context of Isaiah's prophecy, Jesus was talking about replanting after the uprooting of the exile. This is confirmed as Jesus quotes Isaiah: "To you has been given the secret of the kingdom of God, but for those outside everything is in parables, so that 'they may indeed see but not perceive, and may indeed hear but not understand, lest they should turn and be forgiven'" (Mark 4:10–12; cf. Matt 13:11–16; Luke 8:10; see Isa. 6:9–10). These verses have baffled many readers. Is Jesus deliberately confounding his listeners by telling parables? Is he concerned that if they understood, they might turn and be forgiven? Jesus then goes on to say, "Do you not understand this parable? How then will you understand all the parables?" (Mark 4:13). All becomes clear when we realize that Jesus is quoting Isaiah 6. He is giving a commentary on the return from exile, foretold by Isaiah, that is now happening through his ministry. God is replanting Israel in a new way, through Jesus's ministry. But not everyone accepts this.

Some are like a path, others like rocky or thorny soil. But some, likened to good soil, understand what is happening. If you don't understand this, you won't understand any of Jesus's parables.

As Isaiah continues his ministry, he preaches both the woes of exile and the hope of return. The return is expressed in hyperbolic images of healing and abundance. The blind will see, the deaf will hear, the lame will leap like a deer, the mute will sing for joy, and water will gush in the wilderness, "and the ransomed of the LORD shall return and come to Zion with singing; everlasting joy shall be upon their heads; they shall obtain gladness and joy, and sorrow and sighing shall flee away" (Isa. 35:5–10). Jesus quotes this section of Isaiah, together with Isaiah 61, in a synagogue in Nazareth as he begins his ministry. The homecoming foretold in Isaiah is being realized. We read: "He rolled up the scroll and gave it back to the attendant and sat down. And the eyes of all in the synagogue were fixed on him. And he began to say to them, 'Today this Scripture has been fulfilled in your hearing'" (Luke 4:20–21).

The crescendo of Isaiah comes as we read that the return from exile will lead to the renewal of the heavens and the earth. God's commitment to creation is clear: "For behold, I create new heavens and a new earth" (Isa. 65:17). This renewal of all things will be fully realized at Jesus's return, which will usher in "a new heaven and a new earth" (Rev. 21:1). The return from exile will result in the renewal of creation. The message of Isaiah is clear: we are part of something that is so much bigger than ourselves. The Gospels pick up this message and tell us how the ministry of Jesus is central to this cosmic renewal. A return from the Babylonian exile will happen in the ministry of Jesus that will in turn result in the renewal of creation.

Jeremiah

Jeremiah also wrote from Jerusalem prior to the exile, prophesying the destruction of the city (Jer. 1:14–15) due to its idolatry (Jeremiah 2–9). Judea will face famine and be conquered, plundered, and taken captive to a foreign land (Jeremiah 10–11), but God will bring his people back (Jeremiah 30–33).

The book of Jeremiah is very instructive for how the Israelites were to respond to Babylonian society during the exile. What were they to do while in exile as they awaited their final return? When I was a university student many years ago, the Christian group on campus encouraged me to choose work of eternal significance, most especially some form of full-time ministry in the pastorate or on the mission field. Other types of work would have been fine too, however, because they can be means of support to those in full-time ministry. Many years have passed since those days at university. We now live in a world where public schools are increasingly hostile to Christianity, and where changing medical ethics and the media are at the forefront of the secularization of society. Where are the Christian leaders in these areas of society? Would our society be different if Christians understood their career as an act of Christian service—even in a hostile world? We ought to heed Jeremiah's encouragement to the exiles in Babylon:

> Thus says the LORD of hosts, the God of Israel, to all the exiles whom I have sent into exile from Jerusalem to Babylon: Build houses and live in them; plant gardens and eat their produce. Take wives and have sons and daughters; take wives for your sons, and give your daughters in marriage, that they may bear sons and daughters; multiply there, and do not decrease. But seek the welfare of the city where I have sent you into exile, and pray to the LORD

on its behalf, for in its welfare you will find your welfare.
(Jer. 29:4–7)

Jeremiah's prophesies of homecoming are fulfilled in the ministry of Jesus. Jeremiah says, "Behold, the days are coming, declares the LORD, when I will make a new covenant with the house of Israel and the house of Judah" (Jer. 31:31). In this covenant, God says, "I will put my law within them and I will write it on their hearts" (Jer. 31:33), and, "I will remember their sin no more" (Jer. 31:34). Jesus fulfills these prophecies. He is the High Priest of a new covenant that does not depend on eternal regulations performed by external priests in an external temple. He fulfills everything within himself. He is the temple; he is the High Priest; he is the sacrifice; his is the obedience. When speaking of his impending death, Jesus made reference to Jeremiah to say that this death "is the new covenant in my blood" (Luke 22:20). Jesus is the "mediator of a new covenant, so that those who are called may receive the promised inheritance" (Heb. 9:15). It is Jesus who will finally bring his people home by forgiving the sins that led to exile.

This homecoming, based on forgiveness, was likened by Jesus to the return of a prodigal son from a distant land (Luke 15:11–32). As we noted above, the parable of the sower that talks of Israel's return from exile is a key to understanding all the parables (Mark 4:13). Israel had forsaken its Father and become destitute in a foreign land where unclean pigs were fed but now has returned home and is being reestablished. There were some who recognized their waywardness that had led to exile, and who rejoiced. But many of the leaders of Israel, against whom Jesus told this parable (Luke 15:1–2), did not recognize what was happening and, like the older brother in Jesus's story, did not join in the festivities. Once we understand that Jesus's parables are more about the kingdom of

God than about us, we will see a broader application arising from their original intent.

Ezekiel

As we turn to Ezekiel, we see that the prophet wrote from the perspective of Babylon prior to the exile. The overarching theme of this book is an answer to the question, If the Lord dwells in his temple, what happens if the temple is destroyed? The answer came in the first vision Ezekiel received by the Chebar canal (Ezek. 1:1) in which he saw the throne of God transported to Babylon (Ezek. 1:4–28). God's presence remained with his people despite geographical location. Upon the throne was seated one with the "likeness of human appearance" (Ezek. 1:26). The Hebrew word translated "human" here is the word *'adam*. The Edenic overtones are never far removed. In Babylon, Ezekiel received a vision of the idolatry that was happening in Jerusalem. Women were engaged in the practices of a fertility god Tammuz (Ezek. 8:14), and men were worshiping the sun (Ezek. 8:16). The Lord's response was decisive: "Therefore I will act in wrath. My eye will not spare, nor will I have pity. And though they cry in my ears with a loud voice, I will not hear them" (Ezek. 8:18).

Against this background of idolatry and judgment, we see that God's people needed both cleansing and resurrection:

> I [God] will take you from the nations and gather you from all the countries and bring you into your own land. I will sprinkle clean water on you, and you shall be clean from all your uncleannesses, and from all your idols I will cleanse you. And I will give you a new heart, and a new spirit I will put within you. And I will remove the heart of stone from your flesh and give you a heart of flesh. And I will put my Spirit within you, and cause you to walk in my statutes and

> be careful to obey my rules. You shall dwell in the land that
> I gave to your fathers, and you shall be my people, and I
> will be your God. (Ezek. 36:24–28)

Without this forgiveness, the people remain in exile, despite their geographical location. This cleansing will result in the restoration of God's original purposes in creation: "The land that was desolate will become the garden of Eden" (Ezek. 36:35). Furthermore, the nation in exile needed to be reborn. The nation is likened to a valley of dry bones (Ezek. 37:11) that needs to be brought back to life. God will breathe life into Israel (Ezek. 37:9–10) as he breathed life into Adam (Gen. 2:7). Corporate Adam will be raised from death.

The cleansing and rebirth of Israel happens in the death and resurrection of her Messiah, Jesus. The temple that will be rebuilt is likened to Eden:

> On the banks, on both sides of the river, there will grow all
> kinds of trees for food. Their leaves will not wither, nor their
> fruit fail, but they will bear fresh fruit every month, because
> the water for them flows from the sanctuary. Their fruit will
> be for food, and their leaves for healing. (Ezek. 47:12)

In the light of this, when Jesus said, "Destroy this temple, and in three days I will raise it up" (John 2:19), he was referring to the resurrection of his body (John 2:21) that will usher in the restoration of Eden. In Jesus, the sins of the exile are forgiven through his death, and Israel is reborn through his resurrection.

The trajectory is now set. The promises to Israel are now embodied in her Messiah. The temple is no longer a building. God now indwells his people through the Holy Spirit (John 7:39). Christians are now called the living stones of God's temple (1 Pet. 2:5). Through Israel's Messiah, who acts on behalf of Israel, Israel is brought home from exile. Sins are forgiven.

Israel is raised as those who are joined to Christ, even Gentiles (Rom. 11:17) anticipate the new heavens and the new earth, for which all of creation groans (Rom. 8:22–23). At this point, we will be home. All this has been brought about through the death and resurrection of Israel's Messiah, who brings us home from exile.

7

On the Way Home

The ministry of Jesus occurred within a historical context. We noted in the previous chapter that Jesus's ministry fulfilled the prophetic expectations of a return from the Babylonian exile and that in turn the earth would be blessed. We now turn our attention to the historical context of Jesus's ministry to understand more fully its significance. During the period since the Jewish people had returned from exile in Babylon, much had happened in Jerusalem. Jewish kingdoms had risen and fallen. Different sects of Judaism were teaching different kingdom and messianic expectations. We will begin our survey from the return from the Babylonian exile.

Reconstruction of the Temple

In 537 BC the Jewish exiles in Babylon began to return to the Promised Land following Babylon's defeat by the Persian king Cyrus in 539 BC. In an unexpected turn of events, Cyrus saw himself as having been charged by God to rebuild the temple in Jerusalem (Ezra 1:2; Isa. 44:28). Hence the first wave of exiles, numbering 49,897 (Ezra 2:64), led by a Judean prince named

Sheshbazzar (Ezra 5:14) returned to Jerusalem and laid the foundation of the temple. But work on the temple was soon delayed (Ezra 5:16). The prophet Haggai rebuked the returnees for building their own houses while the house of God lay in ruins (Hag. 1:4, 9). In response to this, Zerubbabel, Sheshbazzar's successor, organized a labor force to continue work on the temple. Haggai reminded the people that God would again reside in the midst of his people:

> I will fill this house with glory, says the LORD of hosts. The silver is mine, and the gold is mine, declares the LORD of hosts. The latter glory of this house shall be greater than the former, says the LORD of hosts. And in this place I will give peace, declares the LORD of hosts. (Hag. 2:7–9)

This prophecy expressed the hope of those who returned from the exile, that the Lord would come to his temple.

The temple was completed in 515 BC, in the sixth year of the reign of the Persian king Darius (Ezra 6:15) and during the time of the prophet Zechariah. The dedication of the temple was cause for much celebration (Ezra 6:16), but unlike the dedication of the former temple built by Solomon, there is no mention of the glory cloud filling it (see 1 Kings 8:10–13; 2 Chron. 5:13–6:2). Is a temple a temple if God does not dwell within it? Had the sins that led to the exile been forgiven? In this context, the prophet Zechariah reminds the people that repentance is more foundational than rebuilding a physical temple (Zech. 1:2–6) and that a messianic king will come, "humble and mounted on a donkey, on a colt, the foal of a donkey" (Zech. 9:9).

King Darius died in 486 BC, and the throne passed to his son Xerxes, who married a Jewess named Esther. The astute reader of the book of Esther can see how much God's people had compromised their distinctive Jewish behaviors during the time of the exile. Unlike Daniel, who at the beginning of the exile was prepared to be thrown to the lions rather than to compromise (Daniel 6), or Shadrach, Meshach, and Abednego, who found themselves in a fiery furnace (Daniel 3), by the time we come to the end of the exile, Esther is the second wife of a Gentile king (Est. 2:17). Esther's name was possibly derived from the Babylonian goddess Ishtar and her cousin Mordecai's name from the Babylonian god Marduk. It appears that the Jews in Babylon had not yet reached a point of repentance for the sins that had led to the exile.

The second wave of returnees from Babylon arrived in Jerusalem in 458 BC, the seventh year of the reign of King Artaxerxes, Xerxes's son (Ezra 7:7). Nehemiah arrived in Jerusalem in 445 BC to rebuild the city walls (Neh. 1:3), which took only fifty-two days to complete (Neh. 6:15). In the newly established city there was confession of sin and rededication to God (Neh. 7:73–10:39), but the Lord still did not return to his temple.

As the Old Testament closes, the people are awaiting the Lord's visitation upon the second temple. Malachi proclaims that this day will come: "Behold, I send my messenger, and he will prepare the way before me. And the LORD whom you seek will suddenly come to his temple; and the messenger of the covenant in whom you delight, behold, he is coming, says the LORD of hosts" (Mal. 3:1; see also Mal. 4:5). We know from the New Testament that this messenger foretold by Malachi is John the Baptist, who prepared the way for Jesus (Mark 1:2; Luke 7:27).

Jews today are still awaiting the Lord's visitation to the temple. They pray constantly at the Western Wall in Jerusalem that the Lord will come to his temple. On the western slope of the

Mount of Olives that overlooks Jerusalem, many Jewish people are buried, believing that on the day of the Lord's visitation, when the dead will be raised, they will be there to welcome him in the temple. Their hope is that the coming of the Messiah will reestablish Israel and thereby bring blessing to the ends of the earth. Christians believe that this has already happened. The Lord has come to the temple. In so doing he has redefined Israel, not as a political entity within geographical borders but as those united to Christ. God's blessings are flowing to the ends of the earth.

After the close of the Old Testament, the power of the Persian kingdom started to decline, and the Greeks gained ascendency. This transition of world empires was confirmed in 333 BC at Issus (modern-day Turkey), when the armies of Alexander the Great defeated the armies of the Persian king Darius III. Alexander went on to conquer much of the known world, from Greece in the north to Egypt in the south and even as far as India in the east. This conquest led to Israel being ruled by Hellenistic kingdoms for nearly two centuries.

Desecration of the Temple

Rule by foreign powers, whether Babylonians, Persians, or Greeks, made no sense to faithful Jews. Had not God elected them to be a light to the nations? Why then were the nations exerting influence over them? This paradox reached its crescendo in the second century BC, when a Hellenistic king, Antiochus IV (of the Seleucids/Syrians), ruled Israel. In 168 BC Antiochus failed in an attempt to conquer Egypt. He returned to his kingdom in a spirit of wild vindictiveness and treated Jerusalem as if it had been the cause of the defeat. He outlawed the observance of the Sabbath, circumcision, and possession of the Hebrew Scriptures. These "crimes" were punishable by death. Jewish worship was abolished, and pagan altars were erected in many of the cities of Judea. The temple was transformed, and an altar to Zeus was placed within it, and in 167 BC a sow (yes, a pig!) was sacrificed on the temple's great altar.

From December 167 to December 164, Judean Jews experienced some of the darkest days in their history. The different Jewish groups united against a common enemy. This resulted in the Maccabean revolt, named after the greatest of the insurrectionists, Judas Maccabeus. The revolt began with Maccabeus's father, Mattathias, a priest. Under the threat of death, Mattathias refused to make a sacrifice to Zeus in the town of Modein. A Jewish man came forward and offered to make the sacrifice instead of Mattathias. This act of compromise enraged Mattathias, who slew the man who had offered to take his place. He then killed the foreign officer and pulled down the altar and, in turn, sparked a widespread revolt.

Mattathias and his followers went up and down Israel, hiding by day and attacking by night. They pulled down pagan altars, circumcised boys, and, as far as they were able, guaranteed safety in the observance of the Mosaic law. Mattathias died in 165 BC. His death is recorded in the apocryphal book of 1 Maccabees, which says, "Now the days drew near for Mattathias to die, and he said to his sons, 'Arrogance and scorn have now become strong: it is a time of ruin and furious anger. Now, my children, show zeal for the law, and give your lives for the covenant of our ancestors'" (1 Macc. 2:49, 50 NRSV). He bequeathed the leadership of the struggle to the third of his five sons, Judas Maccabeus. The Maccabean revolt continued under Judas until after the death of Antiochus IV (164 BC), at which time a truce was finalized between the Jewish rebels and their Hellenistic overlords.

Rededication of the Temple

This truce did not mean political liberation for a Jewish nation, but it did mean religious freedom, and it led to the rededication of the temple after its desecration by the sacrifice of a sow. The purification of the temple is described in 2 Maccabees, and it is worth quoting in full:

> Now Maccabeus and his followers, the Lord leading them on, recovered the temple and the city; they tore down the altars that had been built in the public square by the foreigners, and also destroyed the sacred precincts. They purified the sanctuary, and made another altar of sacrifice; then, striking fire out of flint, they offered sacrifices, after a lapse of two years, and they offered incense and lighted lamps and set out the bread of the Presence. When they had done this, they fell prostrate and implored the Lord that they might never again fall into such misfortunes, but that, if they should ever sin, they might be disciplined by him with forbearance and not be handed over to blasphemous and barbarous nations. It happened that on the same day on which the sanctuary had been profaned by the foreigners, the purification of the sanctuary took place, that is, on the twenty-fifth day of the same month, which was Chislev. They celebrated it for eight days with rejoicing, in the manner of the festival of booths, remembering how not long before, during the festival of booths, they had been wandering in the mountains and caves like wild animals. Therefore, carrying ivy-wreathed wands and beautiful branches and also fronds of palm, they offered hymns of thanksgiving to him who had given success to the purifying of his own holy place. They decreed by public edict, ratified by vote, that the whole nation of the Jews should observe these days every year. (2 Macc. 10:1–8 NRSV)

The waving of palm branches at the rededication of the temple was a sign of victory. The same display was still alive at the time of Jesus as the people of Jerusalem welcomed him as their messianic king, as he headed for the temple to purify it (John 12:13), riding on a donkey. Jews today continue to remember Judas Maccabeus's cleansing of the temple in the Jewish month of Chislev (normally early December) in the festival of Hanukkah.

Judas Maccabeus died in battle in 160 BC. His younger brother Jonathan succeeded him by assuming command of the army, and the military might of the Jews increased. Jonathan was slain in battle in 142 BC and succeeded by the last remaining son of Mattathias, Simon. Under Simon, complete political independence was achieved in 134 BC. Coins were struck bearing his name, and contracts were dated with reference to his rule: "The people began to write in their documents and contracts, 'In the first year of Simon the great high priest and commander and leader of the Jews'" (1 Macc. 13:42 NRSV).

The Jewish state, now thoroughly politicized, began to develop territorial ambitions and conquered Moab, Samaria, and Idumea. This time of political independence for Israel still has significance in the Jewish mind-set and certainly did at the time of Jesus. Within a generation of the Maccabean revolt, those who ruled this politically independent nation were called kings. Was this the kingdom of God? But all was not well within it. Internal divisions continued. Treaties were formalized with Gentile nations, and idolatry continued. Some decried this compromise and protested. They were called the Hasidim, which means "the separated ones," who, by the time of Jesus, had evolved into a sect called the Pharisees. Others withdrew and prayed for the cleansing of the temple. This monastic group became the Essenes. Zealots would say their prayers and sharpen their swords. Others accommodated the political beliefs of the time, which became the mark of the Sadducees. Rising animosity was exhibited between different Jewish groups. This led to a divided kingdom that became easy prey for the rising world power, the Romans, who conquered Judea in 63 BC.

This history is very important for an understanding of Jesus's proclamation of the kingdom of God and its relation to the blessing of the earth. Jewish political kings had risen and fallen prior to Jesus's ministry. When Jesus claimed, "My kingdom is not of this world" (John 18:36), he was referring not to the domain over which he rules but to the origin of his kingdom and the manner in which the kingdom is ruled. Jesus went on to say, "If my kingdom were of this world, my servants would have been fighting that I might not be delivered over to the Jews. But my kingdom is not from the world" (v. 36). Jesus is not saying that his kingdom will have no effect in this world! He is contrasting the origin of his kingdom with the origin of other kingdoms of the world, such as the Maccabees who ruled before him. Jesus's kingdom would not be brought about by political states or by human effort. This message is as relevant now as it was then. The Messiah's role is not to establish an independent state called "Israel." Political Israel was not and is not the path to the establishment of the kingdom of God. Indeed, it is salient to realize that between the exile to Babylon in 586 BC and the formation of the modern state of Israel in AD 1948, there has been an independent Jewish nation only between 142 BC and 63 BC. That is 79 years within a time period of 2,534 years.

By the time we come to the New Testament, we are introduced to a strange combination of kingship and temple embodied in one man—Herod. Herod was not a Jew but an Idumean, Idumea being one of the areas annexed to Israel in the Maccabean times. The Romans had appointed Herod as their puppet ruler under Roman domination. This was not the sort of kingship the Jews wanted, and it led to a period of significant unrest.

Herod's life was a contradiction as he sought to appease both the Romans and the Jews. His private life was extremely unsavory: he killed two of his ten wives, at least three sons, a brother-in-law, and a wife's grandfather. His propensity for bloodshed is seen in his command after he heard of the birth of the "king of the Jews" (Matt. 2:2), that all the male children two years old or under in Bethlehem be slain (v. 16). Bethlehem was a small town, and the number of infants slaughtered may not have been great, but numbers were of little consequence to the parents whose sons were killed. Herod built temples in honor of the Roman emperor Augustus at Samaria (Sebaste), at Caesarea Maritima, and at Paneion (Caesarea Philippi). Yet simultaneously Herod sought to ingratiate himself to the Jews. He enlarged the Jerusalem temple, which was the most noteworthy of his many building projects. Sometimes the completed temple is called "Herod's temple" or the "third temple," but such designations lack accuracy. It was an extension of the second temple built by Zerubbabel. The development began in 20 BC, and Herod hoped that he would be remembered by the Jewish people with eternal gratitude for this work. It was completed in AD 63 and destroyed by the Romans in AD 70. It stood for less than a decade!

All these grandiose projects needed money. Herod was also required to pay taxes to Rome for the privilege of receiving Roman protection. Herod levied poll taxes, land revenues, and sales taxes. The collection of these taxes was delegated to tax collectors. It is into this fractured world of looking for the Lord's visitation upon the temple and filling it with God's glory that the Lord Jesus was born. The people were not satisfied with Herod's building works. They longed for God to establish his kingdom among them.

Visitation of the Temple

Within each of the Gospels we read that the Lord did come to his temple. It happened in the ministry of Jesus. But upon arrival at the temple, Jesus wept. He said of Jerusalem, "You did not know the time of your visitation" (Luke 19:44). As he entered the temple, he cursed a fig tree, and after he left the temple his disciples noted that the tree had withered (Mark 11:13–14, 20). Israel had not borne fruit. A new temple had arisen. The Lord had come to his temple. He had cleansed it of the moneychangers (Matt. 21:12; Mark 11:15; John 2:15). He had spoken of the end of unfruitful Israel. Worship and fruitfulness will be seen in a new temple: the Lord Jesus and those who are grafted into him. He is the mediator between heaven and earth.

In AD 66–70 the Romans waged war on the Jews. The temple was razed to the ground, as Jesus had foretold (Luke 21:5–6) with not one stone remaining. Today's Western Wall is not part of the original second temple; it is part of Herod's development around the temple. The Jews were driven from the land. Spoils were carried to Rome, and coins were minted with the words *Iudea Capta*, which means "Judea conquered." It would appear from this that the Gentiles had captured and conquered Israel, but Israel was instead redefined as those who had union with Christ. It was not a kingdom of this world like that of the Maccabees, but it did have power. In time the gospel influenced even the Roman Empire.

In AD 312, the Roman emperor Constantine, at the Milvian Bridge in modern-day Italy, acknowledged the higher reign of King Jesus. The following year he issued the Edict of Milan, which decriminalized Christianity throughout the empire. Rome surrendered. This development was within the understanding that Christianity was not tied either to a human-built temple or to geographical Israel. The Lord had come to his temple and redefined Israel. As a result, blessings would flow to the nations. Through Israel, fulfilled in her Messiah, the whole earth will be blessed.

8

God's Kingdom, God's Home

As the New Testament opens, the tensions of the closing chapters of the Old Testament and of the intertestamental period remain. The Lord was yet to come to his temple, and Israel was still under foreign occupation. Neither of these things made sense. God had chosen Israel to be the place where he would dwell, and through her to bless the nations and the earth. But the reality was so different. The temple built by Zerubbabel was but a shadow of the glory of Solomon's temple, and Herod's enlargement of it was a mixed blessing. The king of the Jews, Herod, was neither a king nor a Jew. He was a Roman puppet and an Idumean. Where was the long-expected Davidic messianic king? When would God come to his temple? The short-lived days of the Maccabean kings had raised expectations for the establishment of God's kingdom. Had not the Lord announced to King David through the prophet Nathan, "Your throne shall be established forever" (2 Sam. 7:16)?

The Kingdom Is at Hand

Into this context John the Baptist appeared, announcing: "Repent, for the kingdom of heaven is at hand" (Matt. 3:2). Among

John's original audience, many would have understood this proclamation in political terms, others in temple terms, but it is unlikely that anyone would have heard it in twenty-first-century individualistic terms. Few would have seen it as entry to heaven; most would have seen it as heaven's entry to earth. As the pages of the Gospels unfold, kingdom realities are seen in the realm of the spiritual, as evidenced by Jesus's exorcisms, but they are also evident in the realm of the physical as Jesus healed people of diseases and raised the dead. The dualism that is so evident among twenty-first-century Christians who distinguish kingdom work from other work, or who separate the spiritual from the physical, or who value the sacred over the secular, would have been foreign to John's audience.

Two Kingdoms or One?

What is the kingdom of heaven (or, as it is also called, the "kingdom of God")? Are there two kingdoms (one sacred and one secular) or only one? The debate has raged for centuries. An early proponent of this two-kingdom view was Augustine of Hippo, who lived in North Africa. In AD 410 he wrote the great Christian classic *The City of God*,[1] in which he reflected upon how the Christianized Western Roman Empire could fall. It is a question similar to how the people of God could have gone into exile in Babylon. Augustine's answer is that there is a distinction between the city of God and the city of man. The two cities are grounded in two loves: the love of God, which leads to genuine Christian fellowship, and the love of self, which leads to war, strife, and the exercise of dominion over others. In the wake of the fall of Rome, Augustine wrote that the city of man is destined to perish, but God is creating a new city from its ruins.

---

1. Augustine, *Concerning the City of God*, trans. Henry Bettenson (Middlesex, UK: Penguin, 1972).

This new city, the city of God, is seen today as the church. In the meantime, as we await the city of God, God is preserving the city of man by his common grace. This understanding of two cities means that Christians are called to belong to two cities: the city of God, which will endure, and the city of man, in which they live as faithful citizens, parents, children, and friends.

Augustine's two-city approach relativizes the importance of the two realms. The city of man is an earthly city; it is not the city of God. It is Babylon. It is not our home. Like Daniel in Babylon, we are to pray for the city, to work in the city, and to contribute to its welfare, but we are never to forget that we are pilgrims on our way to another city. We are exiles, and our security belongs elsewhere. Christians may choose to work in politics, in medicine, in agriculture, but such secular callings are not integral to the renewal of creation. At best, these careers serve society as we await the city of God.

Augustine's view of two realms did not appear within a vacuum. He was working within a paradigm of Christendom, within which were those who entered monastic orders in pursuit of the kingdom of God, and those who remained in society, the city of man. This understanding of Christendom continued into the Middle Ages, during which time everyone in Western Europe, with the exception of small minorities of Muslims and Jews, belonged to the Roman Catholic Church. Europe was perceived as a Christian continent. In 1302 Pope Boniface VIII issued a bull called *Unam Sanctum* in which he declared that there was only one kingdom, but the church controlled the spiritual sword, and the state controlled the temporal sword. By "sword" he meant compulsion, and the spiritual sword was "higher" than the temporal. The church could therefore exert influence and power over the state. This power led inevitably to corruption.

It was against this backdrop that Martin Luther, an Augustinian monk, and those after him such as John Calvin and the Puritans (including some of the drafters of the First Amendment of the United States of America's Constitution) argued for a two-kingdom view, or what has commonly become known as a separation of church and state. Luther argued that God rules the earthly kingdom through law (i.e., compulsion) and the heavenly kingdom through the gospel of grace.[2] Calvin largely followed Luther's view, although without the divide between law and grace. Calvin argued that Christians are "under a twofold government . . . so that we do not (as commonly happens) unwisely mingle these two, which have a completely different nature."[3] For Calvin, "Christ's spiritual kingdom and the civil jurisdiction are things completely distinct,"[4] but that does not mean that civil jurisdiction is polluted or has nothing to do with Christian people.

It was in the rise of Neo-Calvinism and its most influential proponent, Abraham Kuyper (1837–1920), that the two-kingdom premise was questioned.[5] Neo-Calvinism's one-kingdom view is built upon the the premise that Jesus is Lord over *all* creation. Jesus's lordship is not restricted to areas of church or piety; all of creation is to be redeemed. This idea of the redemption of all creation is the fulfillment of the cultural mandate and refers back to God giving Adam dominion over all creation. Neo-Calvinism rejects any hint of dualism between secular and spiritual spheres. God is concerned for all. It is therefore possible to apply a Christian worldview to any legitimate endeavor.

2. See Paul Althaus, *The Ethics of Martin Luther*, trans. Robert C. Schultz (Philadelphia: Fortress, 1972), 43–82.

3. John Calvin, *Institutes of the Christian Religion*, trans. Ford Lewis Battles, 2 vols. (Philadelphia: Westminster, 1960), 4.20.1–4.

4. Ibid.

5. For a helpful summary of Kuyper's views see Richard J. Mouw, *Abraham Kuyper: A Short and Personal Introduction* (Grand Rapids, MI: Eerdmans, 2011).

This brief historical survey helps us to understand the influence of the two-kingdom view on modern Protestantism. It can be traced back to Luther and Calvin, who were working in an environment of the political excesses of Roman Catholic Christendom. We know that power can corrupt, and many examples of this can be cited from Christendom. But the problem there is sin, not a one-kingdom view. The church no longer exercises such power over society, but many Christians continue to hold dualistic presuppositions: secular and spiritual, laity and clergy, church and state, those in ministry and others who support those in ministry, Sunday and Monday, heavenly and earthly. An extreme example is seen in the preaching of Dwight L. Moody (1837–1899), who said, "I look upon this world as a wrecked vessel. God has given me a lifeboat and said to me, 'Moody, save all you can.'"[6] Such a view has little place for cultural renewal, social action, or political involvement, as the vessel is doomed to destruction. Such a view leads to the often-heard cry that Christian young people should leave their ambitions for a career in teaching, medicine, law, or politics to do something that has eternal significance!

But is that what Jesus taught about the kingdom? Jesus did understand the authority of the state. His opponents marveled when he stated, "Render to Caesar the things that are Caesar's, and to God the things that are God's" (Mark 12:17; cf. Matt. 22:21; Luke 20:25), but this does not mean that the state acts independently of God's ultimate sovereignty. "For there is no authority except from God, and those that exist have been instituted by God" (Rom. 13:1). Jesus did not live in the context of the fall of the Christianized Roman Empire nor in the political context of Medieval Catholicism. Although few would argue

6. Mark A. Noll, *The Old Religion in a New World: The History of North American Christianity* (Grand Rapids: Eerdmans, 2002), 131.

against the idea of the separation of church and state, is this not more a recognition of how power corrupts rather than a theological division of kingdoms?

Your Kingdom Come

Jesus's ministry, as foretold by John the Baptist, was concerned with the kingdom. The word *kingdom* appears 118 times in the Gospels, of which fifty-two use the expression "kingdom of God" and thirty-one refer to the "kingdom of heaven." The difference between the two expressions is normally seen as stylistic, with Matthew preferring "the kingdom of heaven" for his more Jewish audience, who would not utter the name of God. At its core, Jesus's teaching about the kingdom is summed up in the Lord's Prayer: "Your kingdom come, your will be done, on earth as it is in heaven" (Matt. 6:10; Luke 11:2). The prayer is that God's kingdom will come to earth and that God's will be done on earth as is the case in heaven. Earth is spoiled by sin, but the question is whether it is spoiled beyond restoration. Jesus's prayer clearly implies that there is hope.

Any view can be pushed too far and fall into error, and this is true for a one-kingdom cultural mandate view. We may be tempted to think that our commitment to the earth will result in its renewal. This is not what the Bible teaches. Ultimate renewal will not be realized until the time of Jesus's return to earth, and he will do it. But that does not mean that we should not advocate for how it will be then by how that future is anticipated now. This is what New Testament readers refer to as the "now/not yet" tension of the kingdom. What will the kingdom be like? It will be a place of justice, healing, and reconciliation (and many other qualities). Such kingdom values are to be seen in the present as we await the consummation of all things.

The question is, should Christians divide themselves between the kingdom of this world and the kingdom of God? If the answer to this question is yes, it raises all sorts of complications. At what time are they serving which kingdom? Does a Christian politician deal with the kingdom of this world on weekdays and the kingdom of God on Sunday? What kingdom is a mother serving as she cares for her children? How many kingdoms are there? Of course, many theologians who hold to a two-kingdom view do not see things in such black-and-white categories. They see God working in various vocations. But at some point, a line needs to be drawn between the two kingdoms.[7]

The Gospels clearly identify two kingdoms, but the division is not between sacred and secular; the division is between the kingdom of God and the kingdom of Satan. On one occasion, in response to healing a mute man, some people accused Jesus of casting out demons by Beelzebul, the prince of demons (Luke 11:14–15). In response to this charge Jesus said: "Every kingdom divided against itself is laid waste, and a divided household falls. And if Satan also is divided against himself, how will his kingdom stand" (Luke 11:17–18)? The miracles of Jesus are presented as evidence of a battle between two kingdoms: one of God and the other of Satan. Jesus continued, "If it is by the finger of God that I cast out demons, then the kingdom of God has come upon you. When a strong man, fully armed, guards his own palace, his goods are safe; but when one stronger than he attacks him and overcomes him, he takes away his armor in which he trusted and divides his spoil" (Luke 11:20–22). The ministry of Jesus is seen as that which disarms the power of Satan. These two kingdoms continue to exert influence,

---

7. A helpful and balanced example of a two-kingdom view that values work and vocation is G. E. Veith Jr., *God at Work: Your Christian Vocation in All of Life* (Wheaton, IL: Crossway, 2002).

although the kingdom of Satan is defeated. These two kingdoms cannot be divided between sacred and secular. Sadly, the kingdom of Satan is all too evident within the church! But, fortunately, the kingdom of God also exerts its power over all parts of society. Christians know that the kingdom of Satan has been conquered and the strong man (Satan) has been conquered by the stronger man (Mark 3:27), but the effects of sin still abound.

The battle between these two kingdoms comes to the fore in Jesus's trial. In answer to Pilate's question about whether Jesus is the king of the Jews (John 18:33), Jesus answered: "My kingdom is not of this world" (John 18:36). As already noted, Jesus is discussing the origin of his kingdom, not its domain. He does not mean that his ministry is only spiritual or inward, as opposed to that which is seen and tangible. Indeed, at his trial Jesus alluded to the fact that his kingdom is very concerned with the things of the earth. In response to the high priest's question, "Are you the Christ, the Son of the Blessed?" (Mark 14:61), Jesus replied: "I am, and you will see the Son of Man seated at the right hand of Power, and coming with the clouds of heaven" (Mark 14:62). In this reply, Jesus is citing Daniel 7, which says:

> There came one like a son of man, and he came to the Ancient of Days and was presented before him. And to him was given dominion and glory and a kingdom, that all peoples, nations, and languages should serve him; his dominion is an everlasting dominion, which shall not pass away, and his kingdom one that shall not be destroyed. (vv. 13–14)

The dominion that is given to the Son of Man is similar to the dominion that was given to Adam in the garden of Eden. It is dominion over this world. Jesus's repeated use of the title

"Son of Man" (eighty-four times in the Gospels) identifies him as the eschatological king who is the King over all the earth. Jesus restored and expands Adamic dominion.

The two kingdoms we see in the Gospels cannot be divided along the lines of secular and sacred. One has been affected by the fall and the other is from heaven—this is how they are divided. The effects of the fall can be just as sorely felt in the church as in the workplace. Similarly, the effects of the kingdom of God can be lived out on Mondays as well as on Sundays. Jesus is Lord over all. He is committed to his creation. The Son of Man fulfilled all that Adam should have fulfilled, and all that Israel, corporate Adam, should have fulfilled. As we engage in his work, we are involved in the work of the kingdom.

9

The Journey Home

I have learned over the years that although there is only one gospel, which finds its climax in the death and resurrection of Jesus, this gospel is also multifaceted. If you had asked me thirty-five years ago, as a fresh graduate from seminary, to explain the gospel, I would have explained it in terms of guilt and forgiveness. This is an appropriate and correct explanation of the gospel, but is it the only result of Jesus's ministry? The idea of forgiveness resonated with me in my youth as I lived in a world plagued with guilt. But not all people and cultures feel guilt in the same way or to the same degree.

From Guilt and Shame and Fear

Several years after leaving seminary, my family and I moved to Vanuatu (a Pacific Island nation) where I taught in a theological seminary. Shortly after arrival, despite at that stage having neither an understanding of the culture nor fluency in the language, I was asked to speak at an evangelistic event. I accepted the invitation, and I spoke in terms of guilt and forgiveness. I am pleased that God can use my failures, for there was much opportunity for him to use that talk! It did not connect at all. It took me years to work out why. I had moved to a communal culture that worked in categories of shame and honor. Shame is not the same as guilt. Guilt is felt internally by the individual; shame brings dishonor to the family and the tribe. I discovered over time that in that culture a sin is not really *owned* until it is exposed. This forced me to question my understanding of the gospel. Does Jesus's death and resurrection take away guilt or shame? The answer is clearly yes to both. I realized that there is another axis to understanding the same historical events. As I continued to read the Bible, I saw a new richness especially in the letters of Paul, who also lived in an honor/shame culture.

Over years in Vanuatu I grew to know the language and the culture of the people there, and although it is an honor/shame culture, there is an even deeper felt need that is addressed by the gospel—fear. Christians in Vanuatu have been converted from animism, and fear of the spiritual world is alive and well. When people become Christians, they are encouraged to take their "tabu stones" that protect them from the powers of evil and hurl them into the ocean. Even Christians continue to believe that evil spirits can "adopt" physical means to work them harm. A shark attack is not the fault of the shark but of the spirit that has entered the shark. It is normal for Christians who are sick to call the elders of the church to pray for them. If this does not produce the desired outcome, people sometimes call for black magic. I could tell countless stories of how the fear of the supernatural has impacted people's lives.

In that context, so much of the New Testament came alive to me. The Gospels are full of stories about exorcisms and of Jesus driving out fear. I was living in a world in which these stories resounded. Unlike my approach in Australia, where I observed Christians effectively deny the existence of such forces, the people in Vanuatu needed to be reminded of the victory of Christ over such realities. I was left with this question: Is the gospel about the forgiveness of guilt, the release from shame, or about victory amidst fear? The answer is clearly yes to each of those.

Several years have passed since we returned to Australia. The Western world is changing rapidly, to the degree that it is no longer a world of guilt and forgiveness. Moral standards have been relativized. A generation ago, pregnancy out of wedlock invoked guilt, and divorce was seen as shameful. Many of the inviolable ethics of previous generations have been diluted. I doubt that guilt or shame speaks at the same volume to our current generation. Furthermore, with the rise of Western skepticism, fear of the supernatural is not a felt need. But within this context, there is yet another aspect of the gospel that speaks with resounding relevance to our increasingly disjointed society: homecoming. With the fragmentation of the family, the breaking down of traditional community structures, and the rise of individualism, many in society ask what it means to belong. We have a hunger for home. We long to reverse alienation. Does the gospel of the death and resurrection of Jesus address this? As with guilt, shame, and fear, the answer is yes.

Exile in Crucifixion

We have noted in this book that an overarching story of the Bible is homecoming from exile. Exile from the garden of Eden will result in the homecoming to the new heavens and new earth. Within this overarching narrative have been other exiles. There was an exile to Egypt that found its homecoming in God coming to dwell in the midst of his people in the land and dwelling in his temple (2 Chron. 7:1–3). There was then the exile to Babylon, which found its homecoming in the ministry of Jesus. Exile was caused by sin that needs forgiveness, which is found in Jesus's crucifixion, burial, and resurrection. The relationship between forgiveness and homecoming is clearly taught in the parable of the prodigal son (Luke 15:11–32). We are brought home through the Easter events.

Jesus himself experienced exile in the events that surrounded his trial and crucifixion. He was abandoned by his disciples as they fled from Gethsemane (Matt. 26:56; Mark 14:50), by Peter who denied him (Matt. 26:69–75; Mark 14:66–72; Luke 22:55–63; John 18:15–18, 25–27), and by Judas who betrayed him (Matt. 26:14–16, 47–50; Mark 14:10–11, 43–45; Luke 22:3–6, 47–48; John 18:2–3). The exile continued as Jesus was exiled from justice, as he was condemned to death even though his Roman judge found no guilt in him (Luke 23:4; John 18:38), and as he was led to the cross outside the city. Jesus was exiled from the light of human decency as he was jeered and mocked (Mark 15:17–30). The most excruciating exile of all is heard as Jesus cried out, "Eloi, Eloi, lema sabachthani?" which means, "My God, my God, why have you forsaken me?" (Mark 15:34). Questions abound as to how Jesus could have been forsaken by the Father. How could the Trinity be broken? Clearly it couldn't, and it wasn't. God continued to sustain Jesus on the cross. Yet Jesus received the cup of God's wrath (Matt. 26:39; Mark 14:36; Luke 22:42). He went through hell on earth. He died and was exiled to the tomb of Joseph of Arimathea.

Throughout Jesus's trial and crucifixion, the faithfulness of Israel's Messiah is juxtaposed with the faithlessness of those who surrounded him. Jesus was deserted, denied, betrayed, and abandoned. Jesus, by his obedience in both life and death, will succeed where Adam and Israel failed. The first Adam should have obeyed and lived but disobeyed and died. The final Adam, Jesus, obeyed and died so that death might be destroyed and life renewed in his resurrection. Jesus not only taught the ethics of

God's kingdom; he embodied them. He prayed for those who persecuted him (Matt. 5:44; Luke 23:34), forgave his enemies (Matt. 6:13–14; Luke 23:34), and was perfect even as his heavenly Father is perfect (Matt. 5:48). In so doing he redrew the map of true Israel around his person. The grain died and fell to the ground, and now it can be reborn, spring to life, and bear much fruit (John 12:24). Jesus is the light to the world (John 1:9). Through this exile, Jesus will restore Adamic dominion over all the earth.

Hints about Israel's future outward mission to the ends of the earth happen immediately after the crucifixion. The curtain in the temple was torn in two from top to bottom (Matt. 27:51; Mark 15:38). This is the end of the human-built temple being the house of God. It is possible that this tearing of the temple curtain indicates that any person, not just the high priest, can have access to the Most Holy Place on the Day of Atonement each year. This interpretation, however, is unlikely, as in AD 70 the temple was destroyed, and since then no one has had such access. A more likely interpretation is that Jesus's crucifixion has ended all temple-based sacrifice, and the glory of God has departed the temple. The temple is now redefined. Jesus enters the heavenly temple and pours out his Spirit on his people from all nations. Jesus had promised the gift of the Holy Spirit after his glorification (John 7:39).

There is no longer the need for a temple, as Christians have access to the heavenly sanctuary through the merits of their crucified, risen, and ascended Lord. When Christians gather, God is present as the "living stones are being built up as a spiritual house, to be a holy priesthood, to offer spiritual sacrifices acceptable to God through Jesus Christ" (1 Pet. 2:5). The church becomes an outpost of heaven, as believers are seated with

Christ in the heavenlies (Eph. 2:6). Our lives are hidden with Christ (Col. 3:3). Our citizenship is in heaven (Phil. 3:20). Our treasure is in heaven (Matt. 6:19–21). The Christian hope is laid up for us in heaven (Col. 1:5). All this is because Jesus is in heaven. Worship is no longer centered in Jerusalem. The temple curtain was rent, and God's presence is no longer confined to one physical location. No longer do we make a pilgrimage to the temple, for God's Spirit has been given. Israel is no longer drawn on a map but is now defined as all those who are united with Christ. Through this new Israel, the church, the wider culture is blessed. At Jesus's baptism, the heavens were rent and the Spirit came down upon Jesus. Through Jesus's death, resurrection, and ascension, the Spirit is now given to the church, and thereby blessings flow to the nations.

The beginning of this outward focus of the benefits of the death of Jesus is heard in the words of a Roman centurion. Mark's Gospel begins with the words, "The beginning of the gospel of Jesus Christ, the Son of God" (Mark 1:1). As the reader proceeds through the Gospel, only evil spirits recognize Jesus's identity as being the Son of God (Mark 3:11; 5:7). But at the point of his death, the first human to recognize Jesus's divine identity, in Mark, is a Roman centurion who utters, "Truly this man was the Son of God!" (Mark 15:39). Whether or not this man understood the significance of what he said, Mark places this statement as the first human recognition of Jesus's identity in his Gospel. The man is a Gentile Roman! The outward focus of the kingdom of God is beginning.

The story of the crucifixion concludes with darkness. Creation had done the unthinkable to its Creator. As we read of darkness covering the land (Mark 15:33), it would be good to remember that darkness is not an entity. Darkness is the absence of an entity called "light." An act of "un-creation" was happening. Darkness was the state of pre-creation (Gen. 1:2) prior to the first day of creation when God said, "Let there be light" (Gen. 1:3). This darkness is God withdrawing his light from the world in judgment (Amos 8:9; Joel 2:10, 30–31; Zeph. 1:15). But God has not given up on his creation. From this act of judgment will come a new creation. The first day of creation was the first day of the week. The first day of the new creation was also the first day of the week—resurrection Sunday.

Homecoming in Resurrection

The climax of each of the Gospels is Jesus's resurrection. The way we read the resurrection will impact the way we read the Bible, and vice versa. Many Christians today will say that the resurrection means that they will go to heaven when they die. At one level that is true, but if that is the only answer, it is to miss so much of the significance of the event. After all, the resurrection was not about Jesus being raised to heaven; he was raised to earth where he appeared to many for forty days. As we previously noted, it is important not to confuse the resurrection and the ascension. The resurrection is about the homecoming of the final Adam to the earth that ushers in its renewal and gives meaning to legitimate activity on earth.

The Old Testament foresaw a resurrection that focused more on Israel than on individuals. Some Old Testament passages do refer to the resurrection of individuals (e.g., Job 19:25–26; Isa. 26:19; Dan. 12:1–3), but the major thrust deals with the postexilic renewal of Jerusalem, the rebirth of Israel (Ezek. 37:1–14), and the new heavens and new earth (Isa. 65:17). "As such, 'resurrection' was not simply a pious hope about the new life of dead people. It carried with it all that was associated with the return from exile itself: the forgiveness of sins, the reestablishment of Israel as the true humanity of the covenant god, and the renewal of all creation."[1]

In the resurrection of Jesus, this future and culminating point of history has entered into current history. This is illustrated in the dialogue between Jesus and Martha following the raising of Lazarus. Martha gives her understanding of Lazarus's resurrection when she says, "I know that he will rise again in the resurrection on the last day" (John 11:24). But Jesus points out in his reply that this eschatological reality is manifest within history: "I am the resurrection and the life" (John 11:25). The resurrection becomes the firstfruits of all that would follow (1 Cor. 15:20, 23). It was the final vindication for which Israel had been waiting: the exile was over, sins were forgiven, Israel was renewed in a covenant relationship with God, and the blessings flowed to the ends of the earth.

It is important to note that resurrection is not to be confused with immortality. When Paul addressed his Greek audience in Athens in Acts 17:16–34, many scoffed at him because of his teaching on the resurrection. This was not because Greeks did not believe in life after death. Many did. It was because they had no category for the resurrection of the same physical body that was buried. After his resurrection, Jesus convinced his disciples that he was the same Jesus who had been crucified. The Gospel writers emphasize the senses of touch (Luke 24:39; John 20:27) and sight (Matt 28:6; Luke 24:39; John 20:27) and even taste as Jesus eats food (Luke 24:41–43). Thomas recognizes the wounds of Jesus's hands and side (John 20:27). The biblical teaching of resurrection embodies so much more than immortality.

Sadly, in my experience Christians still wrestle with a wrong belief about the resurrection. We affirm the resurrection in the

---

1. N. T. Wright, *The New Testament and the People of God* (London: SPCK, 1992), 332.

creeds, but we often interpret it as immortality. Do we understand the resurrection of our physical bodies and of the physical earth? We are brought home through the death and resurrection of Jesus in the renewal of our home. The sin that led to exile is paid on the cross. Israel is reborn in the resurrection. The renewal of all things is guaranteed through Jesus's physical renewal. Our home will be renewed, and our resurrected and transformed bodies will live here. The gospel forgives our sin, removes our shame, vanquishes our fear, and brings us home. We should not lose sight of any of these dimensions. We are people of the resurrection.

10

An Expanded Home

Churches can be found today on every inhabited continent of the earth. They look different—they reflect diverse cultures, use different languages, and embody an array of traditions. We take this for granted, but the diversity within the church is the result of a movement from the exclusivity of Judaism defined by the works of the law, the temple, and the land to the inclusivity of all the nations of the earth. The gospel breaks beyond physical borders. New wine cannot be contained in old wineskins. The Acts of the Apostles shows this transition from Jewish particularity to worldwide expression. Acts begins with a small group of 120 Jewish Christians meeting in Jerusalem (Acts 1:15); the book ends with the gospel being preached in Rome, the capital of the ends of the earth.

To the Ends of the Earth

So what has changed as we move from ethnic Israel to the church? The answer is, everything and nothing. Everything changes in that the people of God are no longer defined by their physical descent from Abraham nor by Jewish works of the law such as food laws and circumcision. It now all centers upon Christ. Jesus has fulfilled all that pointed toward the coming of the Messiah. Israel is now defined by the Messiah. But nothing has changed. God's people have always understood their commission from the task that God gave to Adam: to bless the earth and to have dominion over it (Gen. 1:28). In Christ, the final Adam, God's purposes in and for creation are fulfilled. In him, "all the families of the earth shall be blessed" (Gen. 12:3).

The reestablishment of Israel begins with the resurrection of Jesus. On one occasion after the resurrection, Jesus was walking with two men on the road to Emmaus. The despondency of these two men was almost palpable as they uttered, "We had hoped that he was the one to redeem Israel" (Luke 24:21). The risen Lord Jesus then explained to them how the Easter events had fulfilled all that the Old Testament had taught. "Beginning with Moses and all the Prophets, he interpreted to them in all the Scriptures the things concerning himself" (Luke 24:27). Israel is redeemed and renewed in the resurrection of Jesus.

This outward focus is a new step. Jesus's ministry during his lifetime had been focused on ethnic Israel. When a Canaanite woman from Tyre and Sidon pleaded for her daughter to be healed, Jesus answered her: "I was sent only to the lost sheep of the house of Israel" (Matt. 15:24). When a Roman centurion asked for his servant to be healed, Jesus marveled at the faith of this Gentile in comparison to the faithlessness of Israel. He exclaimed, "I tell you, not even in Israel have I found such faith" (Luke 7:9). Apart from these two examples of Gentile faith, Jesus's ministry was focused on Israel. The reason for this should be clear from earlier chapters: God's blessings to the world would flow from the election of Israel, but before this could happen, Israel had to obey God's requirements. This obedience would be realized through Israel's Messiah.

Renewed Israel

When Jesus died on the cross, he carried the sins of Israel with him. When Jesus rose again, so did a renewed Israel, not confined by geography or ethnicity. This is the obedience that will lead to God's blessings reaching to the ends of the earth. The church finds its source in Israel, but its mission is to all the nations of the earth. This pattern is repeated in Acts as the book begins with Jewish Christians in Jerusalem (Acts 1–7) before the gospel goes to the nations. Similarly, when Paul traveled to a new city on his missionary journeys, he visited the synagogues first (Acts 13:5, 14; 14:1; 17:1–2, 10; 18:4, 19) before turning to the Gentiles. This is not just a pragmatic strategy because Jews knew their Bibles better than Gentiles. It was a theological conviction that salvation is from the Jews (John 4:22; Rom. 1:16; 2:9) and that there was a divine priority in how this should happen. It showed that the church was the new Israel, comprised of Jews and Gentiles grafted in together through the work of Jesus (Rom. 11:17–24).

This renewal of Israel is reinforced early in Acts by the election of Matthias to be one of the apostles (Acts 1:24–25). With Judas's death there needed to be a replacement so that the number of the apostles (twelve) would correspond to the number of the tribes of Israel. These apostles knew that the resurrection would result in some kind of renewal for Israel, but when they asked, "Lord, will you at this time restore the kingdom to Israel?" (Acts 1:6), they were probably still thinking in ethnic and geographical categories. Jesus's reply shows that the new Israel will break such boundaries. He said, "You will receive power when the Holy Spirit has come upon you, and you will be my witnesses in Jerusalem and in all Judea and Samaria, and to the end of the earth" (Acts 1:8). By the time we arrive at the end of Acts, the church has spread from Jerusalem to many places within Asia and Europe and possibly also to Africa following Philip's encounter with an Ethiopian (Acts 8:26–39).

If the renewal of Israel begins with the resurrection (cf. Ezek. 37:11–14), it is sealed on the day of Pentecost (Acts 2:1–47). Pentecost was an established feast of Judaism that dated back to the time of the exodus from Egypt. It was called Pentecost (from the Greek word for "fifty") as it happened after a week of weeks from Passover (7 x 7 + 1 = 50). The festival happens in late spring to celebrate God's provision through harvest (Ex. 34.22; Deut. 16:9–10). Harvesting was hard work, especially in the ancient world where the only machinery was a knife and sickle powered by human sweat. When the feast of Pentecost arrived, there was a feeling of exhaustion from labor and of satisfaction from the barns being filled. The feast is thus a paradox of emptiness through exhaustion and fullness through provision. The parallel to how the disciples felt having lost their Lord through death yet receiving the Holy Spirit is not too difficult to see.

The outpouring of the Spirit on the day of Pentecost was the clinching evidence that the last days had arrived (Joel 2:28–32; Isa. 32:15; 44:3; Ezek. 36:27). This will be a time when God's blessings will flow to the nations. This was seen as Peter rose to address those who had gathered. Although they were all Jews, they had come from many parts of the Jewish diaspora, and they represented different languages and cultures. As Peter spoke, he was heard in many languages simultaneously. This gift of tongues is clearly miraculous. I know many people who can speak several languages, but none of them can speak them all simultaneously!

Some would say that the breaking down of the language divisions at Pentecost was the reversal of Babel. I think such an interpretation misses the point of what was happening. If it were the reversal of Babel, only one universal language would have been heard. But linguistic diversity remained. Language is both the mirror and the determiner of culture, and those at Pentecost retained their linguistic and cultural diversities, yet the curse of Babel was gone. In this way it was not the reversal of Babel but its redemption. Cultural and linguistic diversity may be a result of sin, but its redemption is not beyond God's purposes. In the same way that healing is dependent on the existence of sickness, which is a result of the fall, and forgiveness has the prerequisite of sin, and reconciliation requires discord, so God takes that which is the result of sin and works it for good. Pentecost embraces cultural and linguistic differences. Even within Jerusalem, within a Jewish audience, we are receiving hints of the diverse nature of the new Israel. Amidst this diversity, a new community of Christians is established that is marked by generosity and commitment (e.g., Acts 2:42–47).

As the story of Acts continues to unfold, the church's mission is given further definition through the interaction between Word-based ministries of proclamation and caring ministries of mercy and compassion. A good example is seen when an issue arose between the Hebraic and the Hellenistic widows in the daily distribution of food (Acts 6:1). This was a real issue of mercy, dealing with people's physical needs across a cultural and linguistic divide. The solution was to appoint seven men, full of the Holy Spirit (Acts 6:3), to minister to these physical needs so that the apostles could devote themselves to the Word and prayer (Acts 6:4). This may fit well into a common modern paradigm of some being involved in "gospel" ministry, and others supporting them from more secular work. But the text of Acts throws a curve ball in the next two chapters that takes us off guard.

The next two chapters of Acts focus on the growth of the church (Acts 6:7), not solely because of those who were set apart for the ministry of the Word and prayer but more particularly because of two of the seven men who were chosen to wait on tables: Stephen and Philip. Stephen gave one of the clearest articulations of the message of Christ that we find in the New Testament. He was not *just* a table waiter. He understood the fulfillment of the temple in the ministry of Jesus. Stephen's teaching was so clear that it cost him his life, and the ensuing persecution of Christians led to Christianity spreading beyond Jerusalem (Acts 8:1; 11:19). Philip became a missionary to Africans. Through an encounter with an Ethiopian official on the Gaza road, he was able to show the connection between a servant song from Isaiah and the ministry of Jesus. The Ethiopian was converted, baptized, and sent on his way rejoicing (Acts 8:36–39). Philip was not *just* a table waiter. He was an evangelist and a biblical scholar. Do those who are given the ministry of waiting on tables have a less important role than those who are set apart for the ministry of the Word and prayer? Do we recognize the important vocation of Christian waiters in our congregations?

The outward focus of the book of Acts, which began in Jerusalem and ended in Rome, gives a lot of space to the evangelization of the Gentiles. A leader in this ministry was the apostle Paul, who was a most unlikely convert to Christianity. We read that Paul (formerly known as Saul) was present at the stoning of Stephen (Acts 8:1). His purge of the emerging Christian religion in Jerusalem succeeded in breaking up the church through the imprisonment, beating, or execution of many members, with the result that Christians were put to flight. Paul's journey to Damascus was in pursuit of adherents of the new faith (Acts 9:2). But the believers of Damascus were unmolested, as Paul's conversion en route to the city marked the subsidence of the storm.

The encounter with the ascended Lord Jesus on the road to Damascus turned Paul's world around. It revealed several truths to him. At the most basic level, it showed him that Jesus, who had been crucified, was now alive. This very same Jesus was so connected to the Christians who were the object of Paul's crusade that he said: "Saul, Saul, why are you persecuting me?" (Acts 9:4). But the encounter moves on from accusation. In this context Paul learned about the forgiving and transforming power of grace.

For Paul, the story of Israel and the story of Christ are interconnected. Jesus was born to redeem those under the law (Gal. 4:4), a clear reference to Israel. Paul understood the Jewish source of the Christian message (Rom. 9:5), but he saw his primary field of activity as being with the Gentiles (Acts 9:15). As the story of Acts proceeds, we see that Paul experienced widespread rejection from the Jews (Acts 13:45, 50; 14:19; 17:5; 18:12; 21:27; 23:12) but a warmer reception from the Gentiles (Acts 13:48; 17:4). Paul understood that the effects of Christ's ministry had brought reconciliation between Christian Jews and Gentiles (Eph. 2:11–22), but also that its effect was felt even beyond Jews and Gentiles. The whole of creation groans awaiting renewal (Rom. 8:20–22). Paul could even write of Jesus's victory over the powers of evil (Col. 2:15). It is within these contexts that the drama of Israel's renewal through her Messiah and the new Christian communities' mission to bless the earth are played out. God's story is interwoven with the world's story. Jesus was the final Adam (1 Cor. 15:21–23, 44–49) through whom God would reconcile all things to himself (Col. 1:15–20).

Blessing the Earth

This understanding of blessing the earth needs a new awakening in the modern church. It is a simple truth that when people become Christians, it changes them, which should bring about change in all they do. New communities are formed. Society is impacted. Churches come to realize that the work of ministry is not just inward in its focus, with the congregation support-ing the church's programs; it is also outward, with the church supporting the members of the congregation to be distinctively Christian in their respective roles. It is good for every church to think about whether it has the right balance between an inward focus of being supported and an outward focus of supporting. A good barometer is to listen to the prayers and announce-ments in church, as well as how the preaching is applied. Do we encourage our people to be committed to the church's activi-ties, or is the church committed to the lives of members of the congregation in their workaday world? Hopefully the answer is both, but it is good for every church to ask if it has the balance right. There are only twenty-four hours in a day, and we need to be responsible in how we use them.

Paul is concerned to impact society. When he arrived in Ath-ens he began his ministry in the synagogue (Acts 17:17), but he did not finish there. He brought his Christian worldview to bear on the Areopagus (Acts 17:19), a center of learning, and to the marketplace (Acts 17:17). He understood Athenian culture as he cited the Greek poet Epimenides (Acts 17:28), and he even appealed to the Athenians' sense of the divine by arguing from creation (Acts 17:24–29). This built an apologetic bridge without allowing any concession to Hellenistic pagan-ism. Giving a defense of the faith is so much more than just transferring knowledge from one brain to another. Knowledge is incarnated and enculturated. As Western society moves away from its Christian moorings, we need to remember not to dis-parage views with which we disagree. We engage with the views around us with a confidence that the gospel not only redeems people but also blesses culture and society. There are many examples in the history of the world. The church is central to this as it sends out its members every Sunday to engage in the world in which we live.

Paul is concerned that churches bless their communities. He commends congregations for how their works are evident to the cities in which they live (Phil. 2:15; Col. 4:5–6; 1 Thess. 4:11–12; Titus 2:9–10). It is a question that every church should ask: Are we blessing the communities in which we live? Are our lives so transformed by the power of the gospel that our workplaces, families, marriages, friendships, and world are improving? Do we understand that the resurrection was physical and that God is concerned for this physical world? Asked another way, if our church were to close down, would anyone in our neighborhood notice the difference?

11

Away from the Body, at Home with the Lord

Among the core beliefs of the Apostles' Creed, we affirm, "I believe in the resurrection of the body and the life everlasting." In this affirmation are we making one statement or two? Is the resurrection of the body the same as the life everlasting?

The Resurrection of the Body

We have noted throughout this book that resurrection is always physical. Bodies do not survive outside of a physical world. Jesus's resurrected body stood on earth with gravity, breathed the air of the atmosphere, and ate food. There is an interdependence between the resurrection of the body and the renewal of the earth. The resurrection of our bodies will not happen until the Lord's return and the renewal of all things.

This raises obvious questions. What is the state of those who have died in Christ and who are awaiting the resurrection of the body? Do we believe in "the life everlasting" that is not interrupted by death? Does the Bible affirm Christians go to heaven at the point of death while their bodies remain in graves? The New Testament answers this important pastoral issue with the comfort that those who have died in Christ are "away from the body and at home with the Lord" (2 Cor. 5:8). For the Christian, life is not interrupted by death.

There is an urgent need for those who preach at funerals to be clear on the relationship between the resurrection of the body and the life everlasting. I have heard ministers at funerals talk of the deceased now enjoying a body that is free of disease and infirmity. This may bring comfort to the bereaved, but it is not grounded in biblical truth, and it removes the future hope of the resurrection. Too often at funerals, I hear a denial of the power of death for the Christian. This is both untrue and pastorally insensitive. Death brings deep grief, even for Christians. Grief is the cost of having loved. Death has great power. The resurrection is not a denial of the power of death but an affirmation of its defeat.

The Christian hope is firmly grounded in the resurrection of Jesus that assures us of the renewal of all creation at the return of Christ. Paul writes, "We know that the whole creation has been groaning together in the pains of childbirth until now. And not only the creation, but we ourselves, who have the firstfruits of the Spirit, groan inwardly as we wait eagerly for adoption as sons, the redemption of our bodies" (Rom. 8:22–23). But in the very same chapter, the apostle also affirms our immortality. Nothing will separate Christians from God's presence. "For I am sure that neither death nor life . . . nor anything else in all creation, will be able to separate us from the love of God in Christ Jesus our Lord" (Rom. 8:38–39). The apostle cries, "Maranatha," which means "Our Lord, come!" (1 Cor. 16:22), but he also states, "For to me to live is Christ, and to die is gain" (Phil. 1:21). How does Paul's teaching on immortality relate to his teaching on the resurrection? What is the hope of the Christian in the face of death? To answer these questions, we will look at three letters written by the apostle: 1 Thessalonians and 1 and 2 Corinthians.

The record of Paul planting the church in Thessalonica is found in Acts 17:1–10. After three Sabbaths reasoning in the synagogue, some Jews and many God-fearing Greeks were persuaded of the truth of Christianity. Paul's ministry in Thessalonica, however, was cut short by a riot that broke out in the marketplace that resulted in Paul making a hasty departure for Berea. Much of what Paul wanted to share with the Thessalonians remained untaught. Confusion arose about what would happen if they died prior to the return of Christ. Had they forfeited the blessings they would have received at Christ's return? Therefore the apostle wrote to them when he arrived in Corinth in AD 50–51:

> We do not want you to be uninformed, brothers, about those who are asleep, that you may not grieve as others do who have no hope. For since we believe that Jesus died and rose again, even so, through Jesus, God will bring with him those who have fallen asleep. For this we declare to you by a word from the Lord, that we who are alive, who are left until the coming of the Lord, will not precede those who have fallen asleep. For the Lord himself will descend from heaven with a cry of command, with the voice of an archangel, and with the sound of the trumpet of God. And the dead in Christ will rise first. Then we who are alive, who are left, will be caught up together with them in the clouds to meet the Lord in the air, and so we will always be with the Lord. Therefore encourage one another with these words. (1 Thess. 4:13–18)

This passage informed the Thessalonians that death would not rob them of participation in the resurrection, as "God will bring with him [Jesus] those who have fallen asleep" (1 Thess. 4:14). Bring them from where? There appears to be some form of existence with Christ after death and prior to the general resurrection. It would appear from this letter that Paul expected to be alive at the time of the coming of Christ. He says, "We who are alive, who are left until the coming of the Lord" (1 Thess. 4:15). Of course, expectation is not the same as apostolic knowledge. Paul declared his ignorance about the time of Jesus's return in the same letter: "For you yourselves are fully aware that the day of the Lord will come like a thief in the night" (1 Thess. 5:2). If Jesus did not know the time of his return (Matt. 24:36), neither did his apostle, Paul.

The anticipation of being alive when Jesus returns continued as Paul wrote his first letter to the Corinthians. This was penned about four years after the Thessalonian correspondence in AD 55. Like much of the Greco-Roman world, Corinth was influenced by Platonism, which, while holding to the continual existence of the soul after death, independent of the body, believed that the perceptible world is not the real world. Reality exists beyond the senses in a world of forms, of which this world is but a copy or image. Platonists determine whether a building has been built correctly by whether it conforms to the plans. They will then ask whether the plans are drawn correctly by whether they accurately reflect what is in the architect's head. The reality is therefore the idea, not the final product. Similarly the body is not the reality of a person's existence; it houses the true essence of the person that cannot be defined by the senses. For the Platonist, death of the body means release of the soul from its physical incarceration. Bodily resurrection was totally foreign to this Hellenistic worldview.

When Paul addressed the council of the Areopagus in Athens concerning the resurrection of the dead, he was faced with mockery from some and cautious curiosity from others (Acts 17:22–34). It is from this context that Paul gave his teaching in 1 Corinthians 15 about the resurrection of the body. Paul was not a Platonist. He stated, "If Christ has not been raised, your faith is futile and you are still in your sins" (1 Cor. 15:17). This is not a mere assertion about life after death; it is a clear statement about the physical resurrection of Jesus.

The resurrection of Jesus is the firstfruits of the harvest that will follow (1 Cor. 15:20, 23). Our bodies will be raised, yet Paul goes on to point out that there will be both continuity and discontinuity between our current bodies and our resurrected bodies. Paul likens the relationship between the two as between a seed and a plant (1 Cor. 15:37). Both a seed and its plant have the same DNA despite the visible transformation. There is both continuity and discontinuity between the perishable body that is laid in the ground and the imperishable that will be raised (1 Cor. 15:42). The discontinuity is expressed by what kind of body it is: "It is sown in dishonor; it is raised in glory. It is sown in weakness; it is raised in power. It is sown a natural body; raised a spiritual body" (1 Cor. 15:43–44).

Care should be taken to understand what is meant by a "spiritual body." Greek can differentiate the substance from which a body is made from that which empowers a body. Paul refers to "spiritual" as that which empowers the body, not as its substance. A steam train is not made of steam, nor is an electric kettle made of electricity, and a gas oven is not made of gas. It is a real body in continuity and discontinuity from that which was buried. This body will be received when Jesus returns. "Behold! I tell you a mystery. We shall not all sleep, but we shall all be changed, in a moment, in the twinkling of an eye, at the last trumpet. For the trumpet will sound, and the dead will be raised imperishable, and we shall be changed" (1 Cor. 15:51–52).

We now turn our attention to 2 Corinthians. Something happened in the short time lapse between 1 and 2 Corinthians that resulted in a change in Paul's expectation surrounding death. Most New Testament scholars date 1 Corinthians in AD 55 and 2 Corinthians in AD 56. In the interim, Paul had a near-death experience that rattled him. He writes: "We do not want you to be unaware, brothers, of the affliction we experienced in Asia. For we were so utterly burdened beyond our strength that we despaired of life itself. Indeed, we felt that we had received the sentence of death" (2 Cor. 1:8–9).

Between Death and Resurrection

Any brush with death changes our perspective on life. The older we get, the less likely it is that we will be alive at the time of Christ's return. A change in expectation is not a change in theology. Paul's understanding of the time of the general resurrection remains firmly at the return of Christ. In 2 Corinthians he writes, ". . . knowing that he who raised the Lord Jesus will raise us also with Jesus and bring us with you into his presence" (2 Cor. 4:14). But the imminence of death is also seen as he writes of how "our outer self is wasting away" (2 Cor. 4:16). He then addresses the state of the believer between death and resurrection in 2 Corinthians 5:1–8 in a series of metaphors.

Paul begins his explanation of the state of the Christian between death and resurrection with a metaphor of temporary and permanent housing. He writes, "We know that if the tent that is our earthly home is destroyed, we have a building from God, a house not made with hands, eternal in the heavens" (2 Cor. 5:1). In speaking of the destruction of this earthly tent, Paul is speaking about death. That which is temporary will be rolled up like a tent, but the new resurrection body is permanent. This resurrection body is received at the return of Christ.

Paul's second metaphor about the state of Christians between death and resurrection is clothing, a metaphor he mixes with the former metaphor of housing. He writes:

> In this tent we groan, longing to put on our heavenly dwelling, if indeed by putting it on we may not be found naked. For while we are still in this tent, we groan, being burdened—not that we would be unclothed, but that we would be further clothed, so that what is mortal may be swallowed up by life. (2 Cor. 5:2–4)

The English translation "further clothed" literally means "overclothed." Paul longed to put on a new set of clothes without taking off the current set. In the context, this is clearly his desire to put on the new resurrection body without taking off his current body. Death is not a certainty for all of us. Should we be alive at the time of Christ's return, we will be overclothed with our new resurrection body without passing through death. But what if death does come first? What if Paul were to take off one set of clothes (his body) but not be overclothed with another? He would be naked. Bodiless. This is a situation from which he recoils. The use of the Greek word for *naked* (*gymnos*) is significant. Platonists longed for a bodiless existence, which was described in terms of nakedness, when the soul is liberated from being clothed with a body.[1] But Paul sees the ultimate Christian hope not in terms of Platonic bodiless existence but in resurrection. Sadly, much of what I have heard about what happens to Christians beyond death has more in common with Platonism than with biblical Christianity.

---

1. See Plato, "Gorgias 524D," in *Plato in Twelve Volumes*, vol. 3, *Lysis, Symposium, Gorgias*, trans. W. R. M. Lamb, Loeb Classical Library (Cambridge, MA: Harvard University Press, 1975), 523. See also Plato, "Cratylus 403B," in *Plato in Twelve Volumes*, vol. 4, *Cratylus, Parmenides, Greater Hippias, Lesser Hippias*, trans. Harold Fowler, Loeb Classical Library (Cambridge, MA: Harvard University Press, 1975), 71.

Paul now introduces his third metaphor: homelands. There are two homelands: one in the body and the other with the Lord. To be in one is to be away from the other. Paul puts it like this:

> So we are always of good courage. We know that while we are at home in the body we are away from the Lord, for we walk by faith, not by sight. Yes, we are of good courage, and we would rather be away from the body and at home with the Lord. (2 Cor. 5:6–8)

The meaning is clear. After Christians have died, they are away from the body, which perishes in the grave, but at home with the Lord in some sort of bodiless existence. So in the light of this, it is appropriate to refer to heaven as "home" as long as we understand that it will not be our permanent home. We still await the new heavens and new earth.

At this point, questions abound. What does a bodiless existence look like? The short answer is, we are not told. Is the time between death and resurrection to be a process of moral refinement? The answer is clearly no. How can a person be compartmentalized into body and soul? Is that Platonic? The answer is, not necessarily. To view a person holistically does not mean that a separation is not possible. Jesus said, "Do not fear those who kill the body but cannot kill the soul. Rather fear him who can destroy both soul and body in hell" (Matt. 10:28). At the point of his death Jesus committed his spirit to his Father (Luke 23:46), and he could tell the thief on the cross that today he would be with him in Paradise (Luke 23:43). Those in heaven also anticipate the day of Christ's return. Those who have been martyred for the faith cry out: "O Sovereign Lord, holy and true, how long before you will judge and avenge our blood on those who dwell on the earth?" (Rev. 6:10). They long for Jesus's return.

The Resurrection of the Body and the Life Everlasting

We can conclude from this that there are three points on a continuum of time. The ultimate hope for the Christian is the resurrection of the body at Christ's return as we affirm in the words of the Creed: "I believe in the resurrection of the body." But should we die prior to the return of Christ, we will be away from the body and at home with the Lord. We therefore add to our affirmation, ". . . and the life everlasting." As for now, while we live in our current bodies, we are at home in the body but away from the Lord. Our future is secure as God has given us the Holy Spirit as a guarantee (2 Cor. 5:5), so "we walk by faith and not by sight" (2 Cor. 5:7).

This belief in both resurrection and immortality is reflected in some of the great documents of the Protestant Reformation. The Westminster Confession of Faith, written in 1646, states:

> The bodies of men, after death, return to dust, and see corruption: but their souls, which neither die nor sleep, having an immortal subsistence, immediately return to God who gave them: the souls of the righteous, being then made perfect in holiness, are received into the highest heavens, where they behold the face of God, in light and glory, waiting for the full redemption of their bodies.

The Heidelberg Catechism, written in 1563, asks: "How does 'the resurrection of the body' comfort you?" The answer is: "Not only my soul will be taken immediately after this life to Christ its head, but even my very flesh, raised by the power of Christ, will be reunited with my soul and made like Christ's glorious body."

As Christians, we affirm in the Apostles' Creed, "I believe in the resurrection of the body and the life everlasting." Christ has been raised from the dead, and so we boldly cry: "O death, where is your victory? O death, where is your sting?" (1 Cor. 15:55).

12

Arrival at Home

We have discovered within this book a recurring pattern in the Bible of exile and return. At different points in history, God's people forsook their covenantal obligations and were sent into exile, whether to Egypt or Babylon. These exiles were not permanent. Through redemptive figures such as Moses, Joshua, and even Cyrus, God restored his people to the land he promised. This restoration involved not just a physical return but also the forgiveness of the sins that led to the exile. These returns resulted in specific structures where sins were forgiven: the tabernacle and the first temple after the exile to Egypt, and the second temple after the exile to Babylon. The ultimate fulfillment of relationship that is prefigured in these Old Testament temples is the ministry of Israel's Messiah, Jesus Christ. In his death and resurrection, relationships are restored, and God brings his people home from exile. The motif of exile and return finds expression in several stories in the Bible, such as Jonah, the prodigal son, and Peter's denial and restoration. God is portrayed as just and merciful, the One who delights to bring his people home.

New Heavens and New Earth

The pattern of exile and return finds its culmination in the closing chapters of the last book of the Bible. Adam and Eve were exiled from their home, the garden of Eden, and when we come to the end of the Bible we see many Edenic references. But the restoration of the garden is not an exact replica of Eden. Those who live away from home for many years discover, when they return, that home has become a different place. Nothing stays the same over time. A garden is a place of growth and development, and when we come to this final view of Eden, we are in the middle of a city, the New Jerusalem.

Cities by definition are places of human achievements. They bristle with the activity of commerce, industry, and the arts. We were made creative beings, in the image of our Creator, and there is no surprise that this has led to many developments, especially in cities. But cities are not places of perfect beauty. The effects of sin are all too evident in crime, pollution, and homelessness. Within this city, the New Jerusalem, we find a garden within a city and the redemption of a sinful world. Human achievement is renewed by God's presence within it, as the kings of the earth bring their treasures into it (Rev. 21:24).

Within this story of exile and return, we meet two Adams: the first Adam and the last Adam. The first Adam was given dominion over the first creation, yet through the entrance of sin and resultant exile, much of the good of creation was undone. The last Adam defeated the power of sin through the cross and resurrection. When Satan, the force behind the destructive effects of sin, is finally cast into the lake of fire and sulfur (Rev. 20:7–10), the total restoration will be ready. The new Jerusalem will descend to earth (Rev. 21:2). This is our homecoming.

All of this builds from the fact that God is committed to his creation. The garden of Eden is the prototype of the renewal of all that God has made. Within the garden, Adam was granted dominion, but dominion does not end with Adam. In a very real sense, Noah was a second Adam who was told to "be fruitful and multiply and fill the earth" (Gen. 9:1). We often refer to Jesus as the second Adam, but the New Testament does not. There have been several Adamic figures throughout history. Noah continued dominion over the renewed creation after the flood. We have noticed that Israel fulfilled the role of corporate Adam. Israel's role was to be a blessing to the nations. Within Israel, the tabernacle, the temple, and the Promised Land each had overtones of Eden. This all points to the one who is the *last* Adam (1 Cor. 15:45), who by his resurrection has initiated the renewal of all things. His resurrection is the firstfruits of the renewal of Israel, the renewal of Adamic dominion and the new heavens and the new earth.

Jesus's resurrection changes everything. It forgives the past and assures the future. The resurrection is our guarantee that the wrath of God has been appeased by the sacrifice of Jesus. How do we know that Jesus was a sinless sacrifice? How do we know that in the final moments of Jesus's life, while in excruciating agony, Jesus did not curse God before his death? The answer is clear. God put his seal of approval on the sacrifice of Jesus by raising him from death. The penalty for sin, death, has been paid in full. The resurrection is our bill of release. We cannot change our past, but we can be forgiven. We know this because of the resurrection of Jesus.

The resurrection also assures our future. Death casts a long shadow over life. Its shadow is everywhere: unfinished books, unfinished symphonies, parents suffering terminal illness before their children become independent adults. If this life is all there is, there are no guarantees, and there is a tinge of futility in all our pursuits. I have never understood the custom of allowing prisoners on death row to choose their favorite meal before their execution. Do you really think they will enjoy it knowing what is about to happen after dessert? Death casts a long gloom over all we do if we believe that at the end is only annihilation. What is the point? The same despondency is also seen among many Christians who believe in the annihilation of this current world. But the resurrection shows not only that God's people will be raised, but that God will usher in a new heaven and a new earth. The labors we do in the Lord are not defeated by death but have eternal significance (1 Cor. 15:58). The resurrection brings forgiveness for the past, meaning for the present, and hope for the future.

John's vision of this ultimate renewal of creation is encapsulated here: "Then I saw a new heaven and a new earth, for the first heaven and earth had passed away" (Rev. 21:1). The expression used is a clear reminder of all that God had created: "In the beginning God created the heavens and the earth" (Gen. 1:1). The expression "heavens and earth" is what grammarians call a "merism." A merism takes two extremes and includes everything in between. If you have hot and cold running water, it implies that you also have every shade of warm. If you know the long and the short of it, you know the lot. Therefore, to paraphrase Genesis 1:1 and Revelation 21:1 would be to say, God made everything, and he is going to renew everything: the heavens, the earth, and everything in between.

We need to ask ourselves, In what sense will the new heaven and new earth be new? What does it mean that "the first heaven and earth had passed away" (Rev. 21:1)? There are two words for *new* in Greek. One is the word *kainos*, which means qualitatively new in kind; the other is *neos*, which means something has superseded something else. To illustrate, there are two women each married to a man with an addiction to gambling. The first woman encourages her husband to go to "Gamblers

Anonymous," and through this he overcomes his addiction. The second woman divorces her husband and remarries. Both women say, "I am married to a new man," but they mean different things by "new." In Greek, the first woman would use the word *kainos* for the same husband who has been renewed; the second woman would use *neos* for the husband who superceded the first one. When the Greek New Testament uses the word *new* to describe the merism of the heavens and the earth, it uses the word *kainos*. It is the same heaven and earth, but it is renewed. This world is not discarded.

So what will be renewed? We have noticed throughout this book how sin has marred God's beautiful creation and caused a rift between heaven and earth. The Lord God no longer walks with his people in the garden (Gen. 3:8); he now lives in a high and holy place called heaven, separated from the sin of earth. No longer do we think of the heavens and the earth as united, with everything in harmony. It is divided. The earth is the place where God's will is not done as it is done in heaven. It is a place of oppression, injustice, addiction, resentment, greed, and self-promotion. We long for a day when God "will wipe away every tear from their eyes, and death shall be no more, neither shall there be mourning, nor crying, nor pain anymore, for the former things have passed away" (Rev. 21:4). We long for the renewal of the earth. We long for the rift between heaven and earth to be healed. This rejoining of heaven and earth found prospective fulfillment in the tabernacle, the temple, the incarnation, and the gift of the Spirit, but we await the day of Jesus's return that will consummate all of this.

The New Jerusalem

The descent of the new Jerusalem to earth will heal the rift between heaven and earth. Jerusalem was the place where God dealt with his people's sin in the temple, on the cross, and in the resurrection. It was the place of forgiveness and substitution. This Jerusalem will descend to earth, which is why John can write: "I saw the holy city, the new Jerusalem, coming down out of heaven from God, prepared as a bride adorned for her husband. Behold, the dwelling place of God is with man. He will dwell with them, and they will be his people" (Rev. 21:2–3).

An understanding of creation and new creation being the bookends of the Bible will transform our understanding of what is important. Christian ministry is not just about telling people how to get into heaven when they die; it is also concerned for what happens in this world. Do not hear me wrong. I am very aware that eternity goes on for a very long time—so long that it cannot be measured. Telling people the way of salvation is of foundational importance. Without repentance of sins and submission to the lordship of Jesus, nothing else makes sense. But that is not the end of the story. If we acknowledge that the Christian's hope is the renewal of all things, it gives meaning to life. Christianity is not just about what happens after death. What you anticipate will determine what you prioritize. We pray, "Your kingdom come, your will be done on earth as it is in heaven" (Matt. 6:10), and we long for the day when that will be a reality on earth. We know that we will not bring about God's kingdom on earth. That work belongs to Jesus alone. But we cannot ignore Jesus's priorities.

The picture of the New Jerusalem that descends is of a wonderful bejewelled city that reminds us of twelve precious stones worn by Old Testament priests to remind them of the twelve tribes of Israel (Ex. 28:17–20; 39:4–14). In Revelation these are applied to the new Israel, the church.[1] The renewal of the

---

1. For a discussion on how these stones that represented the twelve tribes of Israel are now applied to the church, see G. K. Beale, *The Book of Revelation*, New International Greek Testament Commentary (Grand Rapids, MI: Eerdmans, 1999), 1079–90.

earth is through the fulfillment of God's purposes to Israel. The New Jerusalem is massive: a cube of 12,000 stadia in each direction. One stadium (the singular of stadia) was, unsurprisingly, the length of a Roman stadium, which was about 607 feet (185 meters). The new Jerusalem is thus 1,380 miles or 2,200 kilometers on every edge. It would not fit in the modern nation of Israel. That is the distance from Jerusalem to Rome, from Sydney to Auckland, from Montreal to Miami. If you put Mount Everest inside the cube, it would look like an insignificant pimple. It is not even 5.5 miles (9 kilometers) tall. The Mariana Trench, the deepest part of the oceans, is only 7 miles (11 kilometers) deep. Numbers in Revelation are more symbolic than literal. The number twelve thousand conveys completeness, being 12 x 1,000. How big is the new Jerusalem? It covers the whole earth. No longer do we talk of the Holy Land, but of the Holy Earth. We often talk of the effects of the fall filling the whole earth, but in Revelation 21 and 22 we are reminded that God's work of redemption also fills the whole earth. Within this new creation, God dwells. The rift between heaven and earth is gone, and Jesus dwells among his people. John reminds his readers: "I saw no temple in the city, for its temple is the Lord God the Almighty and the Lamb" (Rev. 21:22).

What will this renewed world look like? We know there will be both continuity and discontinuity from our current world, but we also know that all creation is dynamic. I doubt that the renewed creation will lack creativity. There has been much progress in human civilization since Adam and Eve. How much of this progress will be seen in the New Jerusalem? Will we continue to sing the hymns of Isaac Watts? Will we read Scripture? Will we live in houses? Will we enjoy an array of cuisine? Cities are places of development, and we can only dream about what will remain. Within this city, I assume, we will continue to be productive and creative. Work has always been part of God's intention for humanity, even before the fall. Fruitful activity gives meaning and purpose to existence.

Within the New Jerusalem is a garden watered by God. There is a river and the tree of life, and no longer is anything accursed (Rev. 22:1–3). Eden is renewed within a city. The river, which is for healing the nations, flows from the very throne of God (Rev. 22:1–2). This image of a garden within a city reminds us of the harmony that should exist between God's provision and human progress. All that we do is dependent on God. In his name and to his glory we work and engage in productive activity (Gen. 2:15).

The crescendo of this teaching of God's presence in this renewed world is in the words "they will see his face" (Rev. 22:4). Seraphim need to cover their faces in God's presence because they cannot look on the face of God (Isa. 6:2). Moses was only allowed to see God's back (Ex. 33:17–23), and Ezekiel was given a vision of the chariot throne of God on which was the "likeness of the glory of the LORD" (Ezek. 1:28). But that which seraphim do not do, that which Moses and Ezekiel did not see, will be open to the people of God. This is a great affirmation of God's presence with his people. This is the culmination of all the times that God revealed himself to his people, whether in the burning bush (Ex. 3:1–6), at the transfiguration (Mark 9:2–13), or walking among the seven lampstands (Rev. 2:1). In the new creation, "they will see his face" (Rev. 22:4).

This is the Christian hope. It is this picture of a renewed earth that motivates us and allows us to see that what we do from Monday to Saturday (and on Sunday!) is to God's glory and has meaning. Changing diapers, cooking meals, designing buildings, fixing plumbing, and mowing lawns can all be done to the glory of God. Our labors are not in vain. Of primary importance is that people are reconciled to God through the death and resurrection of Jesus. Without this saving work of God, death continues to make all that we do meaningless. But for those who are in Christ, an understanding of the resurrection brings purpose to life. Jesus said, "Surely I am coming soon" (Rev. 22:20), to which Christians reply, "Amen. Come, Lord Jesus!" (Rev. 22:20). Meanwhile we live in the light of that which will come.

Conclusion

When Christians die, we often say that they have been called home. This euphemism is good and appropriate as long as we do not misunderstand it. Those who have died in Christ are in heaven; they are away from the body and at home with the Lord (2 Cor. 5:8). It is the place where God's will is done. It is a preferable place to store up treasure as it is protected from the effects of the fall. Moth and rust do not destroy treasure in heaven, and thieves do not break in and steal (Matt. 6:19). Our hope is laid up in heaven (Col. 1:5). In a sense, heaven is portrayed as a storehouse from which will come great blessings. Our citizenship is in heaven, and from there our Savior, the Lord Jesus, will appear (Phil. 3:20). Our home, our citizenship, and our treasure are where Jesus is. All that we have and are as Christians comes from being united with Christ. Jesus is coming again to the earth. Heaven will be our home as we await the Lord's return, but after that we will be in our eternal home—the new heavens and new earth.

Citizenship in Heaven

The metaphor used by Paul about our citizenship being in heaven (Phil. 3:20) is instructive for us as we compare our successive homes: our current home on earth, our future temporary home in heaven, and our renewed, permanent home of a new heavens and new earth. Paul uses this understanding of citizenship when writing to the Philippians. Philippi was a colony of Rome (Acts 16:12). The history of Philippi will help us to appreciate the metaphor.

The assassination of the Roman emperor Julius Caesar at the hands of Brutus and Cassius in 44 BC saw the resurgence of the Roman Republic. Conflict arose between the republican forces and the imperial forces commanded by Mark Antony. This war came to a decisive battle in Philippi in 42 BC. During this battle, the Philippians helped the imperial army. When the emperor's army defeated the republicans, Emperor Octavian, in an act of gratitude, declared Philippi a Roman colony. Free men born in Philippi were declared citizens of Rome. Latin was decreed as the official language of Philippi. Even though the Philippians lived in Macedonia, they were to live as Romans. So Paul in his letter to the Philippians applies the same logic—they are to live as citizens of heaven even while living on earth, and they are to live consciously awaiting the coming of the Lord from heaven. He states: "Our citizenship is in heaven, and from it we await a Savior, the Lord Jesus Christ, who will transform our lowly body to be like his glorious body, by the power that enables him even to subject all things to himself" (Phil. 3:20–21). The transformation of our bodies will happen when Jesus comes again from heaven to subject all things to himself.

Renewed Earth

This earth is our home. Every time we see a rainbow, we are reminded that God has made a covenant with the earth (Gen. 9:13). He is committed to it. So what difference does this make? Clichéd though the answer may be, it makes a world of difference. If the mission of the church is seen as an extension of the mission of God, God's commitment to this world will help us to determine our priorities.

Any understanding of our mission in God's world starts with the recognition that God has given humanity dominion over creation. It started with Adam, God's vice-regent in the garden of Eden, and continued through other "Adamic" figures such as Noah, who lived at the time of the "re-creation" of the flood, and through Israel, which was chosen to be a corporate Adam through whom blessings would flow to the nations. Tragically, each of these Adamic figures failed, to some extent. Sin marred God's good purposes. Despite this, God's purposes to bless the earth have not diminished. He sent the final Adam, Jesus Christ, the image of the invisible God, the firstborn of all creation (Col. 1:15). This final Adam dealt with the problem of sin in his substitutionary death on the cross, and by his resurrection he inaugurated a new era that will culminate in his return to *this* earth.

So why all this misunderstanding about heaven? Why do we think that it is our eternal home? Is it biblically accurate to think of earth as our eternal home? They are good questions, and this book has sought to answer them with a better understanding of the flow of the biblical narrative. The Bible starts with a declaration that all God created is very good (Gen. 1:31). As we have followed the story of the Bible, we have noticed that God has not forsaken his creation. He reaches out again and again to the earth. The Bible is more a story of God coming to us than of us going to him. Again and again God stoops down to meet his creation. As we come to the end of the Bible, we see not a picture of people being transported to heaven or a picture of heaven. We see a picture of the *descent* of the New Jerusalem. We see a picture of new heavens *and* new earth (Rev. 21:1). The heavens and earth that God created (Gen. 1:1) are the same heavens and earth that will be renewed (Rev. 21:1).

What will this renewed earth look like? We are given a clue as the narrative of Scripture moves from one garden in Eden to another garden in the midst of a city—the New Jerusalem. This is an interesting contrast, as it is God who planted the garden in Eden (Gen. 2:8), but throughout history, it has always been humans who have built cities. The fact that our final home is a garden within a city brings together all that God has made with all that humans have achieved. God delights in human beauty and achievement. That is why we sing to God in church! Our God-given gifts resound to his glory through our creativity and activity.

The picture of harmony between God's creation and human achievement is hard to imagine. Human effort is so permeated by arrogance and sin that it is difficult to imagine untainted human achievement. It is true that every part of creation has been affected by sin, but that does not mean that all goodness has been eradicated from God's creation. Noble deeds can still be found, albeit marred by sin. For the purity of the deeds to be found, as with the smelting of gold, the dross must be removed (2 Pet. 3:10). Appropriate human effort will endure in the new heavens and new earth where righteousness dwells (2 Pet. 3:13).

This picture of the enduring nature of purified, human accomplishments is seen in the image of the glory and honor of the nations being brought into the New Jerusalem (Rev. 21:24–27; cf. Isa. 23:18). As the dross is separated from the gold, so will be found the purity of human achievements in music, art, literature, architecture, drama, food, agriculture, craft, and so much more. What will this look like? Questions abound. Will we take our musical ability into the new creation? Will we continue to sing some of the same songs? Will we use current technology, or will we take our knowledge of technical advancements? Why should the new creation not have marvels of engineering? I don't know the answer to these and many similar questions, but we know that there will be continuity from this earth into the next. It is this continuity that gives meaning to so much that we do now. Neither death nor destruction will have the final say and render all of this world's pursuits futile. Our creativity, purged of sinful arrogance, will find a new significance. The garden is in the city. Human effort and divine glory can exist in perfect harmony if the effects of sin are eradicated.

Conversely, not only do our human efforts continue into the new creation, but our future home impacts how we live now. A commitment to the gospel is a commitment to the values of the kingdom of God that will be fully realized at the time of Jesus's return to the earth. We follow in the steps of Jesus, whose understanding of the kingdom led to a life committed to healing, justice, and compassion. This will be manifested differently in various contexts, but at every level, an understanding of a renewed world, purged of the effects of sin, gives shape to the everyday spaces of our everyday lives.

The Resurrection of Jesus

Central to this understanding of a renewed creation is a fundamental tenet of the Christian faith: the resurrection of Jesus. Jesus was raised physically. His bones will not be found during an archaeological dig. The resurrection of the body is so much more than the immortality of the soul. The very same body that was buried is the body that was raised. This is the Christian hope. Our very same bodies will be raised. This earth will be raised. As Jesus was transformed through the resurrection, so too will our bodies, and this earth, but there is also continuation from our current existence to that which we await.

It all comes back to how we understand the resurrection of Jesus. After the resurrection, Jesus ate fish, he was touched, he spoke, and he listened. It is belief in this resurrection that defines the preaching of the early church. It is the resurrected Jesus that needs to be preached to every generation—not least of all to our own lest we lose this central tenet of the faith and replace it with an understanding of immortality that is devoid of resurrection. Earth is our home. We will be raised as Christ was raised, and although we do not know all the details of what this will look like, we know that "we shall be like him" (1 John 3:2). Christianity is a resurrection religion.

The idea of heaven as our eternal home is so pervasive in many churches that it has given rise to some Christians disparaging the things of earth. It has led to valuing the spiritual over the physical. It has divided our world between sacred and secular. It has devalued the arts, ecology, work, social justice, and so many more pursuits. It has elevated ministers and missionaries to a more exalted status than those in other vocations. It has defined gospel ministry in reductionistic categories. It has left us confused about what parts of life bring honor to God and what parts don't. It has left us confused about where Christian proclamation starts and finishes. What do we define as missionary work? If our labor in the Lord is not in vain (1 Cor. 15:58), what parts of life are included in such labor?

We need a more holistic understanding of God's mission in the world. God has bound himself to creation by an unwavering yet not static covenant. It is this commitment that gives a foundation to our creativity and an assurance of the ultimate goal. It is against these parameters that we can measure whether our labors bring glory to God. For the atheist who claims that the world is an accident and its end is unsure, it is hard to measure ultimate value. For the Christian who believes that the world God created will be annihilated, the relative importance of different tasks is normally measured by that which will survive the destruction of the world, which is normally understood to be spiritual realities. But when we understand that the earth was made by God and declared to be very good, and that it will be renewed, and that many of our current achievements will be purged and have eternal significance, the merit of our activites is measured very differently. Such a worldview is holistic and gives so much meaning to so many of our current pursuits.

In all this, we do not underplay the pervasive effects of sin and the need for judgment. The world cannot advance by its own cultural engagement—the foe is too strong. It all depends on the ministry of Jesus. We proclaim the gospel, which is a message about Jesus. This message must be preached. In the light of Christ's return to the earth, we reflect Jesus's care for his people. We long to remove suffering and injustice and death, but we also recognize that in and of ourselves we are powerless to do it. Jesus will do it. We remember that Jesus identified with this world in his incarnation. He paid the price for the problem of sin on the cross. He guaranteed the future renewal of all things in the resurrection. He empowered us for the present in the gift of the Holy Spirit. He will come again. And so we pray: "Come, Lord Jesus." He will renew our home. In the meantime, we proclaim his lordship over every area of life. The task of the church is both to declare the reality of Christ's rule over his creation and to show what it will look like, as individuals, families, and whole societies are renewed by the gospel of the lordship of Jesus.

We are ambassadors of the Lord Jesus, who will bring about this renewal. And because of him, we are confident. We know that all will be renewed in this place called "home."

General Index

Abednego, 83
Abraham, 19, 20, 35–36; God's covenant promise to, 62
Adam, 24, 30, 35, 65, 134; covenantal blessings of, 66; dominion of over the garden of Eden, 100–101, 114; link between Adam and Eden as a tabernacle, 51; as a priest in Eden (God's Edenic temple), 50; restoration of Adam's dominion through the death of Christ, 106–7. *See also* fall, the; Israel, as a corporate Adam; Jesus Christ, as the final Adam
"Adamic" figures, 145
Alexander the Great, 84
angels, 54; as having human form, 40–41; improper sexual relations of with human beings, 41–42; rebellious angels, 40; as the sons of God, 40–42
Antiochus IV, 84–85
Apostles' Creed, 123, 131
Augustine of Hippo, view of concerning the kingdom of God, 94–95
authority, vice-regal, 25

Babylon, 77, 83, 133. *See also* Israel, return of from Babylonian exile
baptism, 64–65; baptism of Jesus, 71, 108; baptism of judgment, 65
Beelzebul, 99
berith 'olam (Heb. "everlasting covenant"), 34–35
Bible, the, 46; biblical accounts of world annihilation, 46–47
Boniface VIII (pope), 95

Cain, 40
Calvin, John, 96, 97
Cherubim, 50–51
Christendom, 97; paradigm of in the Middle Ages concerning the kingdom of God, 95
Christianity, 75, 125, 129; decriminalization of by Constantine, 90–91; as a resurrection religion, 148; spread of beyond Jerusalem, 118
Christians, 14–15, 36–37, 49, 75, 84, 96, 117, 131, 136; belief of in evil spirits, 104; belief of in the "life everlasting,"

Scripture Index